LET'S PRAY

FOLLOWING THE EXAMPLE OF JESUS AND THE FIRST CHURCH

DEDICATION

Prayer has the power to unite all cultures, genders, and generations in all nations of the world if the focus is upon the throne of God. As authors we acknowledge the power and ability that Biblical prayer had in our lives and the spiritual impact we can testify about. Therefore, we want to dedicate this work firstly to the revival of prayer within our Every Nation family as a global movement. May prayers arise in the heart of everyone who studies this.

Secondly, we dedicate this to the unity of the global church of Jesus Christ. May this work help prayer to become the central breath of the church of Jesus Christ on earth. We trust that prayer will unite, empower, and invade our churches to fulfil God's purpose and mission on earth.

We want to thank everyone who added value to this work and especially those who faithfully encouraged the putting together of it. Special thanks and recognition to Dr. Larry Lea and his teachings on prayer who has impacted both of our lives. Let our prayers prevail with God.

Authors

Let's Pray is both a gracious invitation to draw near to the living God through prayer and a practical guide on how to do so. In the same way that the world has become much more connected through rapidly developing cell phone technology, Pastors Pieter Coffee and Eric Bapetel show us through God's Word and by His Spirit that we have clear access when we pray in this hour to know the Triune God and to partner with Him in His Kingdom purposes.

Their book is also a useful tool that enables followers of Christ to fulfil the Great Commission to make disciples of all nations. The authors give succinct scriptural guidelines to help Christ followers equip new and even older believers to connect with the Lord, so that they may grow and be strengthened in their faith. This is accomplished not just by praying for the disciples, but by praying with the disciples. A timely book for the coming revival!

Dr. MANNY CARLOS
Dean of Spiritual Life, Every Nation Seminary

We as Every Nation Southern Africa are grateful for two of our pastors, Pieter Coffee and Eric Bapetel, who wrote this resource to help build and establish a biblical culture and understanding of prayer and intercessory ministry. Their passion for prayer and intimacy with God will encourage and equip every believer to have a deeper, more intimate relationship with God. Both authors live out their love and passion for people, and this love is evident throughout their book. Let's Pray will refresh and inspire all who read it.

Eric Bapetel is a dear friend with whom I have had the privilege of walking for more than twenty years. His passion for prayer, and his profound insights on prayer and intercession, continuously provoke me to go deeper in prayer. Through Eric's ministry, my desire and stamina for prayer has grown over the years. Eric has a great ability to activate a desire for prayer and a prayer culture in different environments.

I have also had the pleasure of knowing Pieter Coffee for many years. His relationship with God is inspiring – it is the foundation upon which this book's profound insight into God's Word is built. Pieter Coffee has an unusual ability to combine sound theology with practical application in a way that brings transformation to anyone who reads and applies these biblical truths.

I know that working through this material will have a lasting impact on your relationship with God and your prayer life.

Ps GILIAN DAVIDS
Senior Pastor of Every Nation N1 City, Cape Town, South Africa, and member of Every Nation Apostolic Counsel

---

Eric Bapetel and Pieter Coffee are men of faith, men of integrity and men of their word. Yet, they are not only men of their word, but men of the Word. What runs deepest in both of their lives and is most evident, is that they are men of prayer. Having the joy of knowing them both for many years, I have seen and felt their commitment to pray for the nations of the world, the communities of our region, the churches of our movement and for my family and myself.

The words on the pages of this book are from the hearts of men who "stay awake and watch" with Jesus, choosing to not let their own needs and comforts (or desire to sleep) get in the way of another hour of prayer. Writing out of personal experience and with the Bible open has resulted in a book that is a deeply personal invitation to come closer to the heart of God, as well as a powerful practical aid in our prayer journey. Let's Pray is an invitation into a deeper relationship with the happy recipient of each prayer we pray – God our Father, the Son, and the Holy Spirit. This book will encourage you and equip you in your daily walk with God.

Ps PIERRE SMITH
Senior Pastor of Every Nation Somerset-West, South Africa

INSPIRATIONAL CHRISTIAN STORY

A man's daughter had asked the local pastor to come and pray with her father. When the pastor arrived, he found the man lying in bed with his head propped up on two pillows and an empty chair beside his bed. The pastor assumed that the old fellow had been informed of his visit.

"I guess you were expecting me," he said. "No, who are you?" "I'm the new associate at your local church," the pastor replied.

"When I saw the empty chair, I figured you knew I was going to show up." "Oh yeah, the chair," said the bedridden man. "Would you mind closing the door?" Puzzled, the pastor shut the door. "I've never told anyone this, not even my daughter," said the man.

"But all of my life I have never known how to pray. At church I used to hear the pastor talk about prayer, but it always went right over my head."

"I abandoned any attempt at prayer," the old man continued, "until one day about four years ago my best friend said to me, 'Joe, prayer is just a simple matter of having a conversation with Jesus. Here's what I suggest. Sit down on a chair, place an empty chair in front of you, and in faith see Jesus on the chair. It's not spooky because he promised, 'I'll be with you always.' Then just speak to him and listen in the same way you're doing with me right now."

"So, I tried it and I've liked it so much that I do it a couple of hours every day. I'm careful, though. If my daughter saw me talking to an empty chair, she'd either have a nervous breakdown or send me off to the funny farm."

The pastor was deeply moved by the story and encouraged the old guy to continue on the journey. Then he prayed with him and returned to the church.

Two nights later the daughter called to tell the pastor that her daddy had died that afternoon.

"Did he seem to die in peace?" he asked. "Yes, when I left the house around two o'clock, he called me over to his bedside, told me one of his corny jokes, and kissed me on the cheek. When I got back from the store an hour later, I found him dead. But there was something strange, in fact, beyond strange - kind of weird. Apparently, just before Daddy died, he leaned over and rested his head on a chair beside the bed."

Author Unknown

This was an amazing journey and experience of writing to reveal what I have learned over many years about prayer. As young Christian, prayer for me was unsure and a difficult spiritual discipline to do. Over the past thirty-eight years, God taught me through the input of many mentors and today I am privileged to have a culture of prayer established deeply in my life. I value prayer as a priority and enjoy it as a special time of sharing my first love with God. Jesus is my best Friend and God's covenant is a reality to abide and live in daily. Prayer is powerful but simple, like the unknown author of the previous story said:

"Prayer is just a simple matter of having a conversation with Jesus."

I accepted the invitation of the apostle Peter to draw near to God and I love to interact with Him through prayer. I've learned to distinguish between the different voices we hear every day. I want to extend an invitation to all disciples of Jesus to adhere to the call of the Spirit.

My beloved speaks and says to me: "Arise, my love, my beautiful one, and come away. Songs of Solomon 2:10

Pieter W Coffee

To most Christians, prayer is just a means of having our needs met. Just ask God what you want, and He provides. Voila, you have a "happy" Christian. Nope! That's not it. Prayer is a means of communication with God, and a means of birthing the purposes of God in our lives as well as on the earth. It gives man the power to impact heaven, earth, and hell.

In every child of God is a spiritual giant. Prayer helps to awake that giant. Through prayer and the Word of God, in reading, meditation and application, you are made strong and formidable spiritually to face the challenges of life with confidence.

"...the people who know their God shall stand firm and take action"
Daniel 11:32.

When you win the battle that your flesh (sinful nature) puts up against prayer, you can defeat any situation.

Eric Bapetel

TABLE OF CONTENTS

"Let's Pray" is a "hands on" study guide of the prayer model Jesus provided His disciples with. The best way to teach people these principles is to do it in a 'one to one' relationship or a small group setting. Some things in life are taught, but some things are also caught. Trust the Lord to pour out a spirit of devotion in your heart to seek Him wholeheartedly. Mentorship in prayer is necessary and not something we should run from. Therefore, only through applying these principles by praying regularly as individuals and together with others, will people benefit from it. Plan daily to have a specific time for prayer and use this model to pray. The aim of this resource is to establish an effective and sustainable culture of prayer in the lives of the disciples of Jesus. We can use this model in all kinds of prayer from personal prayer to praying for others and the church in general. The principles remain the same. This booklet is divided into three parts.

Part 1 - titled, **"What is Prayer"** - will help to lay a Biblical foundation and understanding about prayer in people's hearts. Here we are focusing specifically on the importance of prayer in the life of Jesus and the early church.

Part 2 - titled, **"Teach us to Pray"** - is a practical section with short teaching on the Lord's Prayer model which we find in the Gospels. This is what Jesus gave us to follow. Praying through this daily has been the custom of many believers around the world who had great testimonies in following this pattern of prayer. This goes together with the summary "Prayer Card" included in the book to carry with us to use at any time in prayer.

Part 3 - titled **"Help us to Pray"** - is an applicational section and will assist people to pray effectively. This is also a very practical part, and everyone is asked not to take the barriers lightly that may hinder the godly outcome of their prayers. Go and study it in scripture and don't allow the enemy to have any hold on your spiritual walk with God.

God desires that all of us will have many testimonies of answered prayers.

Let's Pray!

INTRODUCTION

It is difficult to imagine our lives without mobile connectivity. There are so many advantages in being connected to the outer world, such as finding support or connecting with friends and family at any given time through technology that we can hardly live without it.

God created mankind with the ability to connect much differently than any other creature and to continuously develop new ways to better their standard of living. To find help today when we're in need of support is so much easier than one-hundred years ago. Help is just a phone call away!

We rely on the promises and quality of different products and sign contracts with technology companies to facilitate these social connections. We agree to use the products of certain manufacturers because we are satisfied with their service. In this way, we build trust and become dependent on them.

Our relationship with God can be illustrated with cell phone technology. Through the presence of the Holy Spirit, we can easily stay connected to the Creator of the world and Lover of our souls without any problems. God is just a prayer away!

'Let's Pray' is a booklet that teaches people how to pray. By applying the principles of this book, every person should be much better informed and equipped to develop a deeper relationship with God. It will assist believers in establishing an effective and sustainable culture of prayer in their lives. Our spiritual growth and trust in God and His Word will increase tremendously through a disciplined prayer lifestyle.

Prayer is one of the spiritual disciplines Jesus taught His disciples and He commanded them to go and teach it to others. Without prayer our spiritual lives are desolate and empty. But through prayer, we not only deepen and ignite our spiritual lives, but also the spiritual lives of others. Let's devout ourselves more and more to God. Remember that- Personal revival is the 'Pacemaker' for Community revival!

The prayer of a righteous person is powerful and effective.
James 5:16b (NIV)

Let's pray!

PART ONE

WHAT IS PRAYER

Chapter 1

What is Prayer?

"Prayer is the most powerful force upon the earth. We have not even begun to tap into the unlimited power available to us through the mighty, prevailing prayer!" Morris Cerullo

Prayer, in Biblical terms, is narrowed down to three key concepts which are supported with promises from God: **asking, seeking, and knocking.**

> *Ask, and it will be given to you; seek, and you will find; knock, and it will be opened to you. For everyone who asks receives, and the one who seeks finds, and to the one who knocks it will be opened. Mathew 7:7-8*

Positioning ourselves in the courtyards of Heaven, allows the Almighty God to intervene in earthly matters. This is what prayer is all about. Asking, seeking, and knocking for wisdom and breakthroughs at the gates of heaven are privileges of the children of God.

Since the Fall of man after which mankind lost their intimate friendship with God, a huge relational distance separated God and man because of sin. Mankind was driven away from God and His holy presence. God set up a cherubim with a flaming sword to guard the way to the Tree of Life. God graciously gave Eve a third son named Seth who was seen as a substitute for Abel. The name Seth means "compensation," and it was as if something was restored to her in the place of Abel. We can say that God heard Eve's prayer.

> *And Adam knew his wife again, and she bore a son and called his name Seth, for she said, "God has appointed for me another offspring instead of Abel, for Cain killed him. Genesis 4:25*

Then after Seth's son Enosh something else was restored and we read about it for the first time in the Bible.

> *To Seth also a son was born, and he called his name Enosh. At that time people began to call upon the name of the LORD. Genesis 4:26*

Ever since, calling upon the name of the Lord was a practice throughout the history of mankind. Not much is said about this action but if we take a deeper look, we will see how it became a custom in the lives of the heroes of our faith, as well as a culture among the people of God. Calling upon the name of the Lord indicates a person's determination to trust God in the days that lie ahead. This is the simplest description of what prayer is: **People calling upon the Name of God.**

Eve received Seth as compensation and the generations after Enosh were brought back and were determined to restore their relationship with God. This is because, from that time onwards people began to call upon the name of the LORD.

If we, like Eve, receive compensation for a lack of something we lost or for the things we have done wrong, we willingly attempt to make the situation better. This is exactly what God did to mankind by sending his son Jesus. Jesus is the only way and Mediator to the Father, and we will not be able to call upon His Name without receiving the gracious gift of eternal life through Jesus Christ.

Abraham, who lived about twenty generations after Seth, followed in this custom of calling on the Name of the Lord. We will see that calling upon the name of the Lord was how people approached God. Many times, they built altars of worship where they sacrificed unto the Lord and reminded Him of His promises. During these intercessions and Godly interventions, a deeper revelation about God was portrayed to mankind. When God's people approached Him in this manner, God would in return connect with them covenantal.

> *Then the LORD appeared to Abram and said, "To your offspring I will give this land." So he built there an altar to the LORD, who had appeared to him. From there he moved to the hill country on the east of Bethel and pitched his tent, with Bethel on the west and Ai on the east. And there he built an altar to the LORD and called upon the name of the LORD. Genesis 12:7-9*

Many years later when Moses was leading the people of God to the promised land, he commanded them to obey God and follow His advice. Here we find another example of prayer.

> *But you who held fast to the LORD your God are all alive today. See, I have taught you statutes and rules, as the LORD my God commanded me, that you should do them in the land that you are entering to take possession of it. Keep them and do them, for that will be your wisdom and your understanding in the sight of the peoples, who, when they hear all these statutes, will say, 'Surely this great nation is a wise and understanding people.' For what great nation is there that has a god so near to it as the LORD our God is to us, **whenever we call upon him**? And what great nation is there, that has statutes and rules so righteous as all this law that I set before you today? "Only take care, and keep your soul diligently, lest you forget the things that your eyes have seen, and lest they depart from your heart all the days of your life." Deuteronomy 4:4-8*

This is a very strong word and commands our attention. Even in the days of the prophet Elijah, he said the following to the Baal priests:

*And you call upon the name of your god, and **I will call upon the name of the LORD**, and the God who answers by fire, he is God. And all the people answered, "It is well spoken." 1 Kings 18:24*

Moses and Aaron were among his priests, Samuel also was among those who called upon his name. They called to the LORD, and he answered them. Psalm 99:6

Many promises are found in the book of Psalms to prove that prayer was also part of David's life and devotion to God. We also see this in the prophetic books.

The LORD is near to all who call on him, to all who call on him in truth. He fulfils the desire of those who fear him; he also hears their cry and saves them. Psalm 145:18-19

They will call upon my name, and I will answer them. I will say, 'They are my people'; and they will say, 'The LORD is my God.'" Zachariah 13:9b

Prayer is like 'glue' that holds everything together; it sharpens our hearts like pencils to better articulate and express our understanding of the mind of God; it fuels the fire of the Holy Spirit and brings revival to our souls. Prayer is not supposed to be an emergency wheel that we use when we're in trouble, but a steering wheel that navigates every aspect of our lives.

In the New Testament this principle of prayer was pivotal in returning to the Lord and in advancing the kingdom of God among the nations.

*For the Scripture says, "Everyone who believes in him will not be put to shame." For there is no distinction between Jew and Greek; for the same Lord is Lord of all, bestowing his riches on all who call on him. For "**everyone who calls on the name of the Lord will be saved**. Romans 10:11-13*

Prayer involved drawing near to God, meeting with the Father, surrendering to Jesus as Lord and King and searching for the presence of the Holy Spirit. Prayer requires us to position ourselves in expectant longing, to seek and connect with our Source of life, as we answer 'yes' to the commands of God.

Prayer is acknowledging the sovereignty of God, while praising Him as we allow the peace of heaven to relinquish (or govern) our anxiety.

Prayer compels us to search for godly solutions to our everyday struggles. It means knocking at heaven's door, opening, and availing ourselves to a dialogue with the Almighty Triune Creator of everything. Prayer reflects the condition of our hearts, and it allows for the tranquillity of God's presence to restore us to His purpose and destiny.

Prayer results in us uniting in our faith with other believers, to intercede against the lost condition of this world caused by sin and disobedience to God. We do this by asking God to intervene in earthly matters. A life devoted to prayer leads to trust being renewed, hope being restored, a forgiving nature, becoming empowered, receiving godly wisdom, and having sincere heart-to-heart conversations with God concerning all matters. Prayer connects the Kingdom of heaven and our will, as we seek God above all else, inviting Him to be exalted above all and allowing the Lordship of Jesus to enter the throne room of our lives.

Prayer anchors the love and goodness of God as our priority, proclaiming that He alone is worthy as we enter His presence and holiness to worship Him. Prayer is the worshipful response of our hearts to our covenant with God, combined with a lifestyle of walking with Him. Prayer is a culture and a natural response for those who love God.

Our hope as God's people is to return wholeheartedly with repentance to Him and position ourselves in a manner that deepens our intimacy with Him so that we may receive His blessing of restoration. When we call on His name, He will hear us and answer our prayer.

> *For you, O Lord, are good and forgiving, abounding in steadfast love to all who call upon you. Give ear, O LORD, to my prayer; listen to my plea for grace. In the day of my trouble I call upon you, for you answer me. Psalm 86:5-7*

"Prayer is the hand that takes to ourselves the blessings that God has already provided in His Son." [1]

"Prayer is the most necessary thing in the spiritual life." [2]

Let's pray!

---

1 Torrey, Reuben A. The Power of Prayer and the Prayer of Power
2 Murray, Andrew. The Master's Indwelling

APPLICATION

Write down three things you have learned from this Chapter:

____

____

____

____

Which truths have you learned that you will commit to apply in your devotion to God:

____

____

____

____

How and in what way will you apply this truth in your daily devotion?

____

____

____

____

Prayer:
Heavenly Father, I thank You for the privilege of approaching You by the blood of Jesus. Let there be divine interventions in earthly matters, as I give myself to a life of prayer. Help me to develop a consistent prayer life and to live closely connected to You. Amen.

Chapter 2

The Heart of Prayer

Prayer is common to everyone and all religions because it's a way of spiritual communication between God and man. Even within false religions and idolatry, prayer is an act of service. Mankind is made in the image of God and as a spiritual being they have a natural desire to connect spiritually with God.

Through prayers we make our request, and we enquire for support and upliftment during times of affliction. Through our prayers, we connect with God to intervene in earthly matters. Through prayers we intercede for friends, family and nations who are lost in their journey with God. Through prayer people can be saved, healed, restored, and forgiven. Prayer enables the power of darkness to be broken and the satanic hold on people's lives to be released.

Prayer establishes our identity in Christ and causes us to become Spirit-empowered when we connect with the Holy Spirit. Praying results in us upholding and deepening our relationship with God. The well-known slogan, *"a family that prays together is a family that stays together"*, is absolutely true when it comes to healthy relationships.

FOLLOW IN THE FOOTSTEPS OF JESUS

As disciples of Jesus Christ, we exist to please our Father. In this journey we have to define our true motivation behind everything we do. In Jesus' teachings to His followers, He was very outspoken about why people do certain things. When it comes to prayer, He touched on two ungodly motivations:

> *And when you pray, you must not be like the hypocrites. For they love to stand and pray in the synagogues and at the street corners, that they may be seen by others. Truly, I say to you, they have received their reward. Matthew 6:5*

> *And when you pray, do not heap up empty phrases as the Gentiles do, for they think that they will be heard for their many words. Matthew 6:7*

These two things are important to notice when we pray; "to be seen by men and to be heard by others" for these are the incorrect motivations for those who follow Jesus. We are called to serve God with pure hearts and upright motivations that will glorify Him only. Jesus' advice to His disciples on how to pray is as follows:

But when you pray, go into your room and shut the door and pray to your Father who is in secret. And your Father who sees in secret will reward you. Matthew 6:6

Our greatest reward in life is to be restored in relationship with God through Jesus Christ; to have eternal life and to be filled with God's peace and power. We should not do anything to be rewarded by God. We deserved eternal separation, but through His grace we were reconciled to Him. He chose us, redeemed us and made us to be royal and holy before Him.

But you are a chosen race, a royal priesthood, a holy nation, a people for his own possession, that you may proclaim the excellencies of him who called you out of darkness into his marvelous light. Once you were not a people, but now you are God's people; once you had not received mercy, but now you have received mercy. 1 Peter 2:9

Let's take a closer look at the prayer-life of Jesus and the first church to discover more about the heart of prayer.

JESUS PRAYED REGULARLY

1. He knew the extent of His dependency on the Father

Jesus is our role model and example to follow. As His ministry demands increased, so did his prayer life! He was a living example of a heart of prayer during His life and ministry on earth. Jesus said:

I can do nothing on my own. As I hear, I judge, and my judgment is just, because I seek not my own will but the will of him who sent me. If I alone bear witness about myself, my testimony is not true. John 5:30-31

2. While He ministered to people

Jesus always prayed during times of ministry

And rising very early in the morning, while it was still dark, he departed and went out to a desolate place, and there he prayed. Mark 1:35

But now even more the report about him went abroad, and great crowds gathered to hear him and to be healed of their infirmities. But he would withdraw to desolate places and pray. Luke 5:15-16

Then children were brought to him that he might lay his hands on them and pray. Matthew 19:13a

3. While teaching and mentoring discipleship

In these days he went out to the mountain to pray, and all night he continued in prayer to God. And when day came, he called his disciples and chose from them twelve, whom he named apostles: Luke 6:12-13

Now it happened that as he was praying alone, the disciples were with him. And he asked them, "Who do the crowds say that I am?" Luke 9:18

Now Jesus was praying in a certain place, and when he finished, one of his disciples said to him, "Lord, teach us to pray, as John taught his disciples. Luke 11:1

4. Before and after performing miracles

And after he had dismissed the crowds, he went up on the mountain by himself to pray. When evening came, he was there alone. Matthew 14:23

So they took away the stone. And Jesus lifted up his eyes and said, "Father, I thank you that you have heard me." John 11:41

5. His life was marked by prayer

During His transfiguration

Now about eight days after these sayings he took with him Peter and John and James and went up on the mountain to pray. And as he was praying, the appearance of his face was altered, and his clothing became dazzling white. Luke 9:28-29

During His suffering and difficult times

And he withdrew from them about a stone's throw, and knelt down and prayed, saying, "Father, if you are willing, remove this cup from me. Nevertheless, not my will, but yours, be done." Luke 22:41-42

Simon, Simon, behold, Satan demanded to have you, that he might sift you like wheat, but I have prayed for you that your faith may not fail. And when you have turned again, strengthen your brothers." Luke 22:31-32

During the institution of the Lord's Supper

Now as they were eating, Jesus took bread, and after blessing it broke it and gave it to the disciples, and said, "Take, eat; this is my body." And he took a cup, and when he had given thanks he gave it to them, saying, "Drink of it, all of you, for this is my blood of the covenant, which is poured out for many for the forgiveness of sins. Matthew 26:26-28

After the resurrection and before the ascension

When he was at table with them, he took the bread and blessed and broke it and gave it to them. Luke 24:30

And he led them out as far as Bethany, and lifting up his hands he blessed them. While he blessed them, he parted from them and was carried up into heaven. Luke 24:50-51

THE EARLY CHURCH PRAYED REGULARLY

The church of Acts followed in His steps and was powerful in prayer and the works of God. As followers of Christ, we are commanded to pray regularly because prayer enables the power of darkness to be broken and the satanic hold on people's lives to be released.

Let's look at how prayer was established in the early church.

All these with one accord were devoting themselves to prayer, together with the women and Mary the mother of Jesus, and his brothers. Acts 1:14

And they devoted themselves to the apostles' teaching and the fellowship, to the breaking of bread and the prayers. Acts 2:42

Now Peter and John were going up to the temple at the hour of prayer, the ninth hour. Acts 3:1

But we will devote ourselves to prayer and to the ministry of the word. Acts 6:4

So Peter was kept in prison, but earnest prayer for him was made to God by the church. Acts 12:5

And when they had appointed elders for them in every church, with prayer and fasting they committed them to the Lord in whom they had believed. Acts 14:23

There is an increasing call of God to His Bride towards their devotion and prayer to Him. He desires more intimacy with His Bride, to walk closer to Him, to be more deeply connected in friendship with Him and to raise more people into a culture of regular prayer.

But know that the LORD has set apart the godly for himself; the LORD hears when I call to him. Psalm 4:3

God has set apart His beloved for Himself, He died for her and paid the full price for his first love. In return, all we should do is to open our hearts and hands and allow Him to lead us in how to walk with Him.

ALL CHRISTIANS ARE COMMANDED TO PRAY REGULARLY

We are called to always pray as followers of Jesus Christ.

Rejoice in hope, be patient in tribulation, be constant in prayer. Romans 12:12

Praying at all times in the Spirit, with all prayer and supplication. To that end, keep alert with all perseverance, making supplication for all the saints. Ephesians 6:18

Do not be anxious about anything, but in everything by prayer and supplication with thanksgiving let your requests be made known to God. Philippians 4:6

I desire then that in every place the men should pray, lifting holy hands without anger or quarrelling. 1 Timothy 2:8

Rejoice always, pray without ceasing, give thanks in all circumstances; for this is the will of God in Christ Jesus for you. 1 Thessalonians 5:16-18

By understanding the heart of prayer, and determining the motivation for prayer, we all can easily commit and start to build a culture of prayer in our lives. Sooner than later, we will find that prayer is like breathing, something we do naturally and without obligation or reminding. God is waiting in anticipation for His people to return to Him and rebuild their lives as a house of prayer.

O you who hear prayer, to you shall all flesh come. Psalm 65:2

A TRIBUTE

One of the most remarkable men in Scotland's history was John Welch, who was born in 1568 and died in 1622. He was the son-in-law of John Knox, the great Scottish reformer. Although he is not as well-known as his famous father-in-law, in some respects, he was a far more remarkable man than Knox. His life is an amazing testimony of grace and mercy. John Welch was a hopelessly extravagant boy, leaving school and his father's house as a teenager and joining the Thieves on the English Border, who made a living by robbing the two nations. Then, after many years, when he was clothed in rags, the prodigal's misery brought him to the prodigal's resolutions, so he decided to return to his father's house. He begged his father to enrol him in college and to give him a chance to prove that he will behave. If he didn't, his father could disinherit him. His father agreed to this. Welch became a diligent student and follower of Christ and eventually entered the ministry.

Most people think that it was John Knox who prayed, "*Give me Scotland or I die.*" It was not, it was John Welch, his son-in-law. John Welch said before he died that he considered the day poorly spent if he did not spend seven or eight hours in secret prayer. After Welch died, an old Scotchman who had known him from his boyhood said of him, "*John Welch was a type of Christ.*" Of course, that was an inaccurate use of language, but what the old Scotchman meant was that Jesus Christ had stamped the imprint of His character upon John Welch. When had Jesus Christ done it? In those seven or eight hours of daily communion with Him. [3]

Let's end this chapter with a description from EM Bounds:

"Persistent prayer is a mighty movement of the soul toward God, and it stirs the deepest forces of the soul toward the throne of heavenly grace. It is the ability to hold on, press on, and wait. Restless desire, restful patience, and strength of grasp are all embraced in it. Prayer is not an incident or a performance but a passion of soul. It is not a want or half-needed desire but a sheer necessity."

Let's Pray!

---

3   Torrey, Reuben A. The Power of Prayer and the Prayer of Power & online research.

APPLICATION

Write down three things you have learned from this Chapter:

____

____

____

____

Which truths have you learned that you will commit to apply in your devotion to God:

____

____

____

____

How and in what way will you apply this truth in your daily devotion?

____

____

____

____

Prayer:
Father God, I pray that You will stir in me a desire for prayer. I pray that You will stir up the hearts of more people across the body of Christ and anoint them with the power of the Holy Spirit, so that they will be passionate about prayer. I pray this in the name of Jesus Christ. Amen.

Chapter 3

The Purpose and Power of Prayer

THE **PURPOSE** AND **POWER** OF PRAYER

THE AUTHORITY OF THE CHILD OF GOD

We find some powerful last words of Jesus about authority, while on earth, in: Matthew 28:18.

All authority in heaven and on earth has been given to me.

These words came as a victory chant from the One who just overcame Satan, sin, sickness, death and all the powers of Hell. It was clear and without any argument that the keys of heaven and hell, life and death are no longer in the hands of Satan but in the hands of Jesus. Equally important is the next two words Jesus said:

"Go therefore ..."

Jesus commanded us to go and execute His authority on earth. This victorious power is executed through the prayer of God's children. We can't pray effective prayers that will bring heavenly breakthroughs without knowing and applying our authority given to us by Christ Jesus.

"Our combat with the devil always should be with the consciousness that we have authority over him in Jesus name, because he is a defeated foe."[4]

Yes, prayer is powerful! It can bring about transformation in every situation and establish victories in life for us in any circumstance. The Bible says, *"they conquered him [Satan the accuser] by the blood of the Lamb and by the word of their testimony."* (Revelation 12:11)

You may ask: What is authority?

Authority is delegated power!

Jesus delegated His authority to us and gave us power over all those of the enemy. Authority is linked to identity, to whom we are in Christ Jesus.

---

4   Quote from: The believer's authority by Kenneth E Hagin Snr.

Behold, I have given you authority [exousia] to tread on serpents and scorpions, and over all the power [dynamis] of the enemy, and nothing shall hurt you. Luke 10:19

We have three mighty spiritual weapons by which we execute His authority through prayer:

- **The name of Jesus**
- **The blood of Jesus**
- **The Word of God**

Our heart's cry should be that the Spirit empowers and trains us to use these weapons effectively in our battles. We have to understand that this power is not in a person's words or the method's that one uses. This power is in the hands of the God we are praying to, the Creator of everything.

Then God said, "Let us make man in our image, after our likeness. And let them have dominion ..." Genesis 1:26a

"I want to focus your attention on two phrases: "let us" and "let them" - and you will agree with me that these two phrases differ from one another. There is a role God played in creation and which He still does; but we as His creature's also have a role to fulfil. The authority to dominate earth was given to mankind only, and prayer involves man giving God the right and permission to intervene in earthly matters." [5]

Prayer activates this divine intervention. God is looking for a people who are connected to the *"Source of life"* to such an extent that His power can flow through them to establish Jesus' rule and reign on earth.

The word *"miracle"* is defined as *"Godly intervention in earthly matters."*

Think about the power of satellite transmission or cell phone connectivity. Think about any electricity supplier who has built a network to channel energy towards people for public use. Through these networks, we are all connected in some way to either people or institutions. One truth stands out in all these examples; - unless we are connected, we will not have the benefit of using this power.

Prayer is a means to connect and remain connected to God without any subscription or further instalments.

---

5 Quote from: Understanding the purpose and power of prayer by Dr. Miles Munroe

Jesus Christ our Mediator has paid the full price and through Him we can live in a powerful intimacy with God Almighty. Submission under His authority is the key. What the global church needs today is not a greater advancement in technology, more innovative organisations, or novel methods.

Rather, it needs highly devoted men and women whom the Holy Spirit can use — prayer warriors that are mighty in the Spirit through prayers.

Prayer activates divine intervention, and the church needs people that execute the authority of Jesus on earth. This starts with small, simple steps of obedience and discipline. Every person can conquer and overcome life's battles through praying. There are however principles to follow and truths that need to be applied in our lives. God is building His church, and His kingdom will stand forever.

> *I will give you the keys of the kingdom of heaven, and whatever you bind on earth shall be bound in heaven, and whatever you loose on earth shall be loosed in heaven. Matthew 16:19*

Jesus commanded His disciples to pray and stated the purpose and power of prayer clearly in one of the parables.

> *And he told them a parable to the effect that they ought always to pray and not lose heart. Luke 18:1*

> *Watch and pray that you may not enter into temptation. The spirit indeed is willing, but the flesh is weak. Matthew 26:41*

We don't have to lose hope or be overcome by temptation. Prayer will prepare and protect us against the forces that work in opposition to our faith. The apostle Paul emphasises the urgency of prayer in his exhortation to the church of Ephesians as soldiers of Christ against the forces of darkness.

> *Praying at all times in the Spirit, with all prayer and supplication. To that end, keep alert with all perseverance, making supplication for all the saints. Ephesians 6:18*

Scripture proves that mankind has the authority and power through the Spirit and will of God to respond to what happens on earth. In fact, God can do anything He chooses, because He is Almighty, but most of His work on earth is done through cooperation with His people.

Even when He wanted to save mankind, He Himself became man in the flesh and through His Son Jesus's death, burial and resurrection, mankind is destined to overcome.

> *And they have conquered him by the blood of the Lamb and by the word of their testimony, for they loved not their lives even unto death.*
> *Revelation 12:11*

The Amplified Bible added the words *"by the utterance of their testimony"* to this scripture above and in the original it means *"by their report"*.

John Wesley said; -
"God does nothing but in answer to prayer."

Prayer is therefore not an option for mankind but a necessity.

> *O you who hear prayer, to you shall all flesh come. Psalm 65:2*

When we pray, heaven can interfere in earthly matters. The church must take up their responsibility anew and return to God in prayerful devotion.

> *If my people who are called by my name humble themselves, and pray and seek my face and turn from their wicked ways, then I will hear from heaven and will forgive their sin and heal their land. 2 Chronicles 7:14*

In closing, let's look at some of the benefits of prayer as well as how it empowers us by focusing on the New Testament in the Bible.

THROUGH PRAYER:

1. We are connecting to God and His Spirit helps us to deepen our relationship with Him.

> *But when you pray, go into your room and shut the door and pray to your Father who is in secret. And your Father who sees in secret will reward you.*
> *Matthew 6:6*

> *Consequently, he is able to save to the uttermost those who draw near to God through him, since he always lives to make intercession for them.*
> *Hebrew 7:25*

Do not be anxious about anything, but in everything by prayer and supplication with thanksgiving let your requests be made known to God. And the peace of God, which surpasses all understanding, will guard your hearts and your minds in Christ Jesus. Philippians 4:6

2. We strengthen the people in the church.

Likewise the Spirit helps us in our weakness. For we do not know what to pray for as we ought, but the Spirit himself intercedes for us with groanings too deep for words. And he wo searches hearts knows what is the mind of the Spirit, because the Spirit intercedes for the saints according to the will of God. And we know that for those who love God all things work together for good, for those who are called according to his purpose. Romans 8:26-28

And so, from the day we heard, we have not ceased to pray for you, asking that you may be filled with the knowledge of his will in all spiritual wisdom and understanding, so as to walk in a manner worthy of the Lord, fully pleasing to him: bearing fruit in every good work and increasing in the knowledge of God; being strengthened with all power, according to his glorious might, for all endurance and patience with joy; giving thanks to the Father, who has qualified you to share in the inheritance of the saints in light. Colossians 1:9

3. We participate in fulfilling His mission to spread the Gospel to the ends of the earth.

You also must help us by prayer, so that many will give thanks on our behalf for the blessing granted us through the prayers of many. 2 Corinthians 1:11

Then he said to his disciples, The harvest is plentiful, but the laborers are few; therefore pray earnestly to the Lord of the harvest to send out laborers into his harvest. Matthew 9:38

4. We are empowered to withstand temptation and the attacks of the enemy.

Watch and pray that you may not enter into temptation. The spirit indeed is willing, but the flesh is weak. Matthew 26:41

5. We support the advancement of the kingdom of God on earth.

Finally, brothers, pray for us, that the word of the Lord may speed ahead and be honoured, as happened among you. 2 Thessalonians 3:1

6. We are built up in our most holy faith and can remain in the love of God.

But you, beloved, building yourselves up in your most holy faith and praying in the Holy Spirit, keep yourselves in the love of God, waiting for the mercy of our Lord Jesus Christ that leads to eternal life. Jude 1:20-21

7. We are relationally reconciled and restored with one another.

Therefore, confess your sins to one another and pray for one another, that you may be healed. The prayer of a righteous person has great power as it is working. James 5:16

8. We enjoy improved physical health.

Is anyone among you sick? Let him call for the elders of the church, and let them pray over him, anointing him with oil in the name of the Lord. And the prayer of faith will save the one who is sick, and the Lord will raise him up. And if he has committed sins, he will be forgiven. James 5:14-15

9. We intercede on behalf of national leaders, kings and influential people and set the bar for harmony and peace to dominate the nations.

First of all, then, I urge that supplications, prayers, intercessions, and thanksgivings be made for all people, for kings and all who are in high positions, that we may lead a peaceful and quiet life, godly and dignified in every way. 1 Timothy 2:1

10. We receive our daily needs from our Heavenly Father.

Therefore I tell you, whatever you ask in prayer, believe that you have received it, and it will be yours. Mark 11:24

And I tell you, ask, and it will be given to you; seek, and you will find; knock, and it will be opened to you. For everyone who asks receives, and the one who seeks finds, and to the one who knocks it will be opened. Luke 11:9-10

WHY PRAYER IS POWERFUL:

Prayer to God through Jesus Christ that is fuelled by the life-giving Holy Spirit, is a mighty weapon given to God's people on earth.

It is embedded in the character and will of God Almighty and the Good News that His Son Jesus Christ brought to the world. Comparing its effectiveness to some elements in creation - it is like an unstoppable wildfire, irresistible as a waterflood, irreversible as a mighty storm, incomprehensible like the radiance of the sun, incessant like monsoon rain, undelayable like birth, indescribable like an eagle's flight, unbound in freedom, as powerful as an earthquake, as invincible as a flash of thunder, ungovernable by any structure, unregulated by any borders, stronger than a fortified iron-barred prison door, as contagious as a pandemic, entering every place, challenging everything, piercing anything and in the end victorious in ability, immovable by any force, untouched by any impossibility, undeniable like truth and immeasurable by any margin.
Holy Spirit empowered prayer is the almighty Voice of God in action.

Let's Pray!

APPLICATION

Write down three things you have learned from this Chapter:

____

____

____

____

Which truths have you learned that you will commit to apply in your devotion to God:

____

____

____

____

How and in what way will you apply this truth in your daily devotion?

____

____

____

____

Prayer:
Heavenly Father, I thank You that I have authority as a child of God. Lord, use my prayers to break the powers of darkness and help establish people in Your purposes. In the name of Jesus, I pray. Amen.

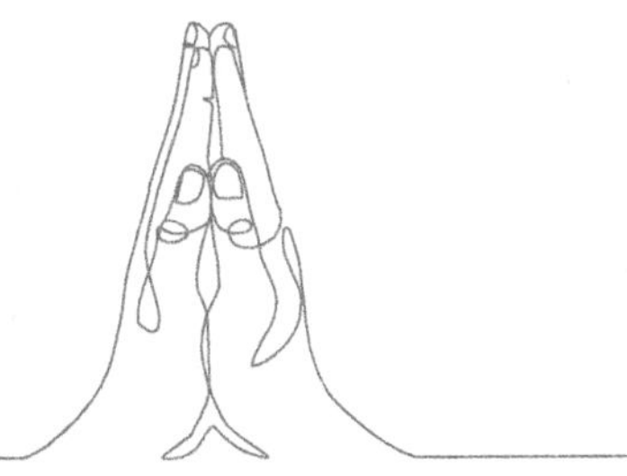

Chapter 4

A House of Prayer

A **HOUSE** OF PRAYER

Jesus cleansed the temple in Jerusalem twice during His ministry on earth. The first time was after the wedding at Cana while the Passover took place in the beginning of His ministry. He made a whip out of cords and chased all the traders out of the temple. He defended the purpose and existence of His Father's house. He accused the traders of misusing what was meant for prayer. The second time, after His triumphant entry in preparation for His suffering, He did the same. (John 2:13-17; Luke 19:45-46)

Paul's letters to the church in Corinth resonates with Jesus's heart and actions:

> *Do you not know that you are God's temple and that God's Spirit dwells in you? If anyone destroys God's temple, God will destroy him. For God's temple is holy, and you are that temple. 1 Corinthians 2:16-17*

All four Gospel writers capture the cleansing of the temple as the house of God. In reading about these events, what should grab our attention is the following (Matthew 21:12-16):

- Jesus cleansed the temple from trading and mentioned that the traders made it a den of robbers. We must live clean lives as temples of God. Jesus has paid the price for us to be holy and to live consecrated unto Him.

- Jesus mentioned that the temple is supposed to be a house of prayer. We are called to prayer and to surrender unto Him. His zeal should motivate us into deeper devotion with God.

- The blind and the lame approached Jesus and He healed them. Signs and wonders followed the cleansing and devotion of the temple.

- The children started to praise Jesus and He referred to this as the fulfilment of prophecy. Our lives will be filled with praise, and pure worship unto Jesus for who He is while many prophecies will be fulfilled in our time.

In view of this, four progressive stages of spiritual growth should be acknowledged in our journey as children of God. We need to aspire to be the following:

1. A HOUSE OF PURITY

Jesus our Bridegroom who is returning soon, longing, and waiting with anticipation to meet His pure and holy Bride. His grace and blood offering cleanses us from all filthiness and empowers us to stand before a holy God. Prayer serves like a broom that cleans our hearts through the confession of our sins.

Blessed are the pure in heart, for they shall see God. Matthew 5:8

For I feel a divine jealousy for you, since I betrothed you to one husband, to present you as a pure virgin to Christ. 2 Corinthians 11:2

So that you may approve what is excellent, and so be pure and blameless for the day of Christ. Philippians 1:10

2. A HOUSE OF PRAYER

In addition to being a house of purity before Him, we should consecrate our whole being to God as a "house of prayer"- a place where He fully reigns as Lord and King. This means a house or temple of holy devotion that exists to honour and serve Him even when sacrifices are required. It is a life declaring His glory and praise wholeheartedly.

Is it not written, 'My house shall be called a house of prayer for all the nations'? But you have made it a den of robbers." Mark 11:17

Then Joshua said to the people, "Consecrate yourselves, for tomorrow the LORD will do wonders among you." Joshua 3:5

3. A HOUSE OF POWER

Jesus called us out of the secular as His church and gave us the power of the Holy Spirit to enable us to be His representatives who execute His authority on earth. Through the presence and power of the Holy Spirit, everything is put in place for believers to be a house of power unto God that advances His kingdom on earth.

But you will receive power when the Holy Spirit has come upon you, and you will be my witnesses in Jerusalem and in all Judea and Samaria, and to the end of the earth. Acts 1:8

And he said to them, "Go into all the world and proclaim the gospel to the whole creation. Whoever believes and is baptized will be saved, but whoever does not believe will be condemned. And these signs will accompany those who believe: in my name they will cast out demons; they will speak in new tongues; they will pick up serpents with their hands; and if they drink any deadly poison, it will not hurt them; they will lay their hands on the sick, and they will recover." Mark 16:15-18

4. A HOUSE OF PRAISE

God is waiting for His worship to be restored in present times. He is worthy to receive our praise. He is a jealous God who does not share His glory with anyone. The more we are filled with His presence, the more glory and praise will be evident in His temple.

I will offer to you the sacrifice of thanksgiving and call on the name of the LORD. I will pay my vows to the LORD in the presence of all his people, in the courts of the house of the LORD, in your midst, O Jerusalem. Praise the LORD! Psalm 116:17-19

What am I to do? I will pray with my spirit, but I will pray with my mind also; I will sing praise with my spirit, but I will sing with my mind also.
1 Corinthians 14:15

Through him then let us continually offer up a sacrifice of praise to God, that is, the fruit of lips that acknowledge his name. Hebrews 13:15

And from the throne came a voice saying, "Praise our God, all you his servants, you who fear him, small and great." Revelation 19:5

RESTORATION OF GOD'S GLORY

The above-mentioned stages can also be seen as stages of the restoration of the tabernacle of God in our midst, the rebuilding of our lives and the establishment of His church on earth.

Simeon has related how God first visited the Gentiles, to take from them a people for his name. And with this the words of the prophets agree, just as it is written, "After this I will return, and I will rebuild the tent of David that has fallen; I will rebuild its ruins, and I will restore it, that the remnant of mankind may seek the Lord, and all the Gentiles who are called by my name, says the Lord, who makes these things known from of old." Acts 15:14-18

A praying church is a preparing church, a church waiting for God to move, a church ready in expectation for His interventions.

The more we cleanse our lives from sin and idolatry, the more He purifies us with His forgiveness.

The more we consecrate our lives through prayer and yield to Him, the more responsive He is to us when we call upon His name.

The more we acknowledge our dependence on Him, the more He will feel compelled to fill us with His power.

The more we turn our affection to Him in praise and worship, the more likely the earthly temples will be saturated with His glory and praise.

These living temples of God don't just have to be restored to their full purpose and destiny; they also need to be revived for the glory of God on the earth.

Let's Pray!

APPLICATION

Write down three things you have learned from this Chapter:

____

____

____

____

____

Which truths have you learned that you will commit to apply in your devotion to God:

____

____

____

____

____

How and in what way will you apply this truth in your daily devotion?

____

____

____

____

Prayer:
Father God, I offer my life as a living sacrifice for Your service and glory. Lord, please restore Your glory in me, because I want to be a house of prayer. Let my life be pleasing to You. Amen.

Chapter **5**

Discipleship and Prayer

DISCIPLESHIP AND PRAYER

DEVOTED TO PRAYER

An ever-present commandment from God is Him calling us, as His church, to pray. Devotion to God should be the essence of every disciple's life. For many of God's people prayer seems like a lost art. The desire to pray is not something we can work up in our flesh. It must be birthed in us by the Holy Spirit as a divine desire implanted into our hearts. Prayer will not come by itself. We need discipleship and mentoring to become a people devoted to prayer.

> *And they devoted themselves to the apostles' teaching and the fellowship, to the breaking of bread and the prayers. Acts 2:42*

Devotion is defined as: **"an intense love and steadfast, enduring loyalty to a person."** It is to **"agree to commit, vowed, and give oneself over."** It may also imply consecration to a cause but devoted to prayer should not be a devotion to a course but to a person.

"Prayer is having an audience with the King of kings, that eternal, omnipotent king in comparison with whom all earthly kings are as nothing."[6]

David desired this and cried out to God for that kind of devotion. Desire and devotion work together, and we find ourselves in a constant tension to balance and direct our desires to God. What and who we value most, will determine our desire in life. Desiring God more than anything else is about having a desire to please Him more than our fleshly desires. A desire to be daily quickened by His love, to stand renewed and unveiled before our Bridegroom. To be filled with His Spirit and to stand clothed and covered with His glory. This should be our priority. Imagine what this will do for our prayer life and spiritual growth. That is why the Bible says the following:

> *Whom have I in heaven but you? And there is nothing on earth that I desire besides you. My flesh and my heart may fail, but God is the strength of my heart and my portion forever. Psalm 73:25-26*

> *For where your treasure is, there your heart will be also. Matthew 6:21*

---

6 Torrey, Reuben A. The Power of Prayer and the Prayer of Power

When looking at how prayer was made a priority in the life and ministry of Jesus, a clear perspective can be observed.

In the beginning of His ministry, we read:

And rising very early in the morning, while it was still dark, he departed and went out to a desolate place, and there he prayed. Mark 1:35.

Towards the middle of His ministry, after many miracles, we read:

And after he had dismissed the crowds, he went up on the mountain by himself to pray. When evening came, he was there alone. Matthew 14:23.

At the end, Luke shares the following about Jesus's prayer life:

"And he came out and went, as was his custom, to the Mount of Olives, and the disciples followed him. And when he came to the place, he said to them, "Pray that you may not enter into temptation." And he withdrew from them about a stone's throw, and knelt down and prayed, saying, "Father, if you are willing, remove this cup from me. Nevertheless, not my will, but yours, be done. And there appeared to him an angel from heaven, strengthening him. And being in agony he prayed more earnestly; and his sweat became like great drops of blood falling down to the ground." Luke 22:39-44

Even on the cross we see Jesus praying, (Luke 23:34, 46). As He died, He cried out: "It is finished!" However, His death did not mark the end of prayer in His life but shows us that His ministry in heaven is a continuation of prayer.

Consequently, he is able to save to the uttermost those who draw near to God through him, since he always lives to make intercession for them. Hebrew 7:25

Jesus has given us His amazing grace by which we are saved and the Holy Spirit to enable us when we pray. Romans 8:26-27

How can we follow in Jesus' footsteps?

How does this desire for prayer start in our hearts?

First, the Holy Spirit births within us the **DESIRE** to pray.

Second, as we obey, desire matures within us and moves into a place of holy **DISCIPLINE** before the Lord. The root word for disciple is 'discipline', and the underlying truth is a disciplined follower of Jesus. Jesus' life was a disciplined life of prayer, and the power of God flowed out of Him.

If we want to see more of the power of God in our lives, there must be a continuous renewal of our relationship with God through a consistent, daily prayer life.

Third, after we discipline ourselves to learn to pray, prayer moves to the third level - from desire, to discipline, to **DELIGHT**. We rejoice and delight in doing His will.

Desire - Discipline - Delight

Discipline is the bridge that links desire and delight. Only through discipline will we be able to reach the delightful celebrations of what we desire. By putting into practice these powerful truths that follow in the next chapters, our prayer life will move from **DESIRE**, to **DISCIPLINE**, to **DELIGHT**.

THE REWARD OF PRAYER

Yes, there is a reward in prayer as already mentioned previously. The Bible teaches us that we should not look for earthly rewards from people when we pray, but instead do the following.

> *But when you pray, go into your room and shut the door and pray to your Father who is in secret. And your Father who sees in secret will reward you.*
> *Matthew 6:6*

Disciplining ourselves to shut the doors of the outer world that influence our trust in the Father in so many ways, will definitely add more energy to our faith when we pray. One day the Holy Spirit asked me this question while praying: *"Who is on the other side of your prayer?"* Do we know Him in such a way that we can fully put our trust in Him? Maybe we can also add; *"What is on the other side of your prayer?"* What is there that may hinder God to fulfil His promises for us? I believe this is crucial to regularly check not just our motives but also what and who influences our faith in prayer. Sometimes we just have to shut the doors that are open to the wrong influence. Withholding God's rewards. The reward is not the secret, the secret is that there is a reward when we pray.

And without faith it is impossible to please him, for whoever would draw near to God must believe that he exists and that he rewards those who seek him. Hebrews 11:6

As we seek Him, we need to put our faith in Him as the source of the reward. I believe the greatest reward is that God hears us and that He will answer our prayers. He is the rewarder of those who trust Him.

SO RUN THAT YOU MAY OBTAIN

Forming a habit of a consistent program of exercise to maintain physical fitness requires discipline and commitment. Forming the habit of a consistent, daily prayer time also requires discipline and commitment. Of Christ's many disciples in the New Testament, perhaps none was more disciplined than the Apostle Paul who wrote these words to the believers at Corinth:

Do you not know that in a race all the runners run, but only one receives the prize? So run that you may obtain it. Every athlete exercises self-control in all things. They do it to receive a perishable wreath, but we an imperishable. So I do not run aimlessly; I do not box as one beating the air. But I discipline my body and keep it under control, lest after preaching to others I myself should be disqualified. 1 Corinthians 9:24-27

In contrasting the athlete and the Christian 'runner', Paul emphasizes the key elements of discipline and purposeful persistence that are essential if the runner is to be victorious. Physical achievement is minor when compared with spiritual victory. Paul is writing to Timothy:

Have nothing to do with irreverent, silly myths. Rather train yourself for godliness; for while bodily training is of some value, godliness is of value in every way, as it holds promise for the present life and also for the life to come. 1 Timothy 4:7-8

If we study the history of the first church in the book of Acts, we find a strong focus and foundation of prayer in every church.

- **When the leaders had to prioritise their focus among all the church activities, they appointed volunteers to serve so that they could focus on prayer.**

    But we will devote ourselves to prayer and to the ministry of the word. Acts 6:4

- **They appointed elders and sent out fivefold leaders after prayer and fasting.**

    While they were worshiping the Lord and fasting, the Holy Spirit said, "Set apart for me Barnabas and Saul for the work to which I have called them." Then after fasting and praying they laid their hands on them and sent them off. Acts 13:2-3

    And when they had appointed elders for them in every church, with prayer and fasting they committed them to the Lord in whom they had believed. Acts 14:23

- **When Paul and Silas were put in jail they prayed, and God miraculously released them.**

    So Peter was kept in prison, but earnest prayer for him was made to God by the church. Acts 12:5

    About midnight Paul and Silas were praying and singing hymns to God, and the prisoners were listening to them, and suddenly there was a great earthquake, so that the foundations of the prison were shaken. And immediately all the doors were opened, and everyone's bonds were unfastened. Acts 16:25-26

- **Paul also encouraged and commanded churches to pray in his Epistles.**

    Rejoice in hope, be patient in tribulation, be constant in prayer. Romans 12:12

    Do not be anxious about anything, but in everything by prayer and supplication with thanksgiving let your requests be made known to God. Philippians 4:6

Throughout the ages, prayer always was a focus of the church of Christ and part of Christian discipline. In almost all churches prayer is a foundational focus as can be seen in the churches of South Korea that have experienced ongoing revival for many years. Let's end off with some of these quotes of well-known writers on the topic of prayer.

"I pray, and I obey."
- David/Paul Yonggi Cho

"It seems God is limited by our prayer life— that He can do nothing for humanity unless someone asks Him."
- John Wesley

"He who is too busy to pray will be too busy to live a holy life,"
- E. M. Bounds

"No man is greater than his prayer life."
- Leonard Ravenhill

Jesus portrayed a lifestyle of prayer in such a way that His disciples urged Him to teach them to pray. If we desire to follow His prayer model, we should allow the Holy Spirit to birth in us a desire to imitate Him wholeheartedly.

One of the main reasons why people struggle to pray is because they don't know how to pray. We must do what Jesus did and disciple people to pray daily.

Let's Pray!

APPLICATION

Write down three things you have learned from this Chapter:

____

____

____

____

____

Which truths have you learned that you will commit to apply in your devotion to God:

____

____

____

____

____

How and in what way will you apply this truth in your daily devotion?

____

____

____

____

____

Prayer:
Heavenly Father, while on earth, Jesus was fully devoted to You in prayer. Help me to develop the kind of prayer life that He had in the days of His earthly life. Lord, I delight in doing Your will and in pleasing You. Amen.

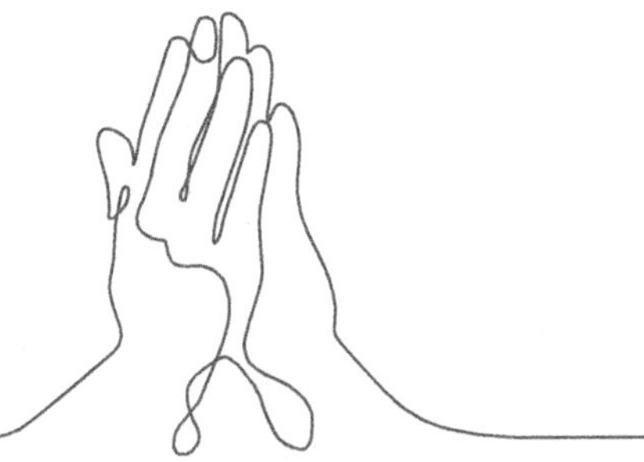

PART TWO

TEACH US TO PRAY

Chapter 6

Jesus' Prayer model

Jesus discipled and mentored twelve hand-picked followers. After three years these disciples expanded to one-hundred and twenty. They were not just taught by Jesus, but they also practiced praying. This is why discipling people in prayer is so important. We should disciple new believers as soon as possible in a lifestyle of devotion and mentor them in prayer. Our prayers are the practical application of what we believe.

Why is it important to follow a specific prayer model when we pray?

One of the best authors on the topic of prayer, E. M. Bounds, said:

"The most important lesson we can learn is how to pray."

Jesus commanded these first disciples to go to Judea and to wait in Jerusalem for the outpouring of the Holy Spirit. (Luke 24:49) What stood out from these first disciples in the Bible was their obedience and commitment to prayer while they waited for the outpouring of the Holy Spirit.

> *All these with one accord were devoting themselves to prayer, together with the women and Mary the mother of Jesus, and his brothers. Acts 1:14*

These disciples had a teachable spirit and among all the questions they could ask Jesus, one of them was that He should teach them how to pray. This shows us how essential prayer was to them. They saw it in the life of Jesus, they remembered that He said He can't do anything without prayer and so they caught a glimpse of the importance of prayer from His life.

> *Now Jesus was praying in a certain place, and when he finished, one of his disciples said to him, "Lord, teach us to pray, as John taught his disciples." Luke 11:1*

Jesus waited to give His disciples a certain model for prayer until they requested it of Him. He gave them clear instructions of what to do when going on a mission, and when discipling others. In the same manner with the same intensity, He gave them specific instructions on how to pray:

Matthew 6:9-13

Our Father in heaven, hallowed be your name.

Your kingdom come, your will be done, on earth as it is in heaven.

Give us this day our daily bread,

and forgive us our debts, as we also have forgiven our debtors.

And lead us not into temptation but deliver us from evil.

[For Yours is the kingdom and the power and the glory forever. Amen!] [7]

WHAT THE LORD'S PRAYER ENTAILS:

We can divide this prayer model into three sections, each with its subdivisions.

Section 1: Focus on God as a person, His authority, and His will.

"Our Father in heaven, hallowed be your name"

The beginning of our prayer commences as we enter God's presence with praise for the blessings and promises provided in the new covenant purchased for us by the blood of Jesus. It immediately turns our affection and focus upwards on God. This is when we acknowledge that He is God, and we are not. In this part of the prayer, our focus is to praise God for who He is.

"Your kingdom come, your will be done, on earth as it is in heaven"

As the prayer continues, in this part, being followers of Christ, we prioritise God's kingdom above our own desires. Our lives revolve around following Him, allowing His Lordship and reign within us. This involves consciously choosing to advance His kingdom above our selfish desires and ideas. This requires us to surrender and submit under His authority. It involves proclaiming that heaven comes down to earth. In this part of the prayer, our focus is to proclaim God's kingdom and will to manifest in our midst.

---

7 This last part of the prayer model in brackets appears only in the King James version of the Bible.

Section 2: Focus on man and the enemy

"Give us this day our daily bread"

In asking God to give us our daily bread, we acknowledge God as a provider and ask for his provision in our lives.

We acknowledge Him as our source and pray for strength and wisdom as we go about our daily lives. We also pray for our spiritual food to keep us spiritually strong to advance God's kingdom and to stay focused on His purpose and destiny for our lives. In this part of the prayer, our focus is to petition for our daily needs through supplication.

"And forgive us our debts, as we also have forgiven our debtors"

This may be the most difficult part of the prayer since it challenges us deep within our hearts. This is where we need to prioritise loving others and to live in peace and harmony with all people. This requires us to pray for reconciliation between all people. It is a time to also intercede for the spiritual and physical healing of people. In this part of the prayer, our focus is to plead or intercede on behalf of ourselves and others before God's throne of mercy and grace.

"And lead us not into temptation but deliver us from evil"

In this section we pray for protection over ourselves, our family, and our possessions and our spiritual family. We prepare ourselves to be victorious in the onslaughts of the devil. We guard our hearts and minds against temptation and the lure of evil. We intercede for those who have enslaved themselves to evil and the lustful things of this world. In this part of the prayer, our focus is to be prepared and protected against the enemy.

Section 3: Focus on worshiping God and victoriously acclaim His glory over us.

"For Yours is the kingdom and the power and the glory forever. Amen!"

We conclude with worship unto the most awesome God who reached out to us first. We proclaim that His kingdom, power, and glory is unstoppable and infinite. In this part of the prayer, our focus is to profess and proclaim God's glory and power over us.

This prayer model provides everything we need to live a full and free life in spiritual victory. The Bible teaches us how to develop an effective and sustainable prayer life - something the church today desperately needs. We are called to align with His power like our forefathers did.

And the prayer of faith will save the one who is sick, and the Lord will raise him up. And if he has committed sins, he will be forgiven. Therefore, confess your sins to one another and pray for one another, that you may be healed. The prayer of a righteous person has great power as it is working. Elijah was a man with a nature like ours, and he prayed fervently that it might not rain, and for three years and six months it did not rain on the earth. Then he prayed again, and heaven gave rain, and the earth bore its fruit. James 5:15-18

Please consider the above-mentioned subdivisions (prayer topics) together with the prayer card as a guide in tracking your daily prayer.

PREPARING YOURSELVES TO MEET WITH GOD

Let's quickly read through the following as a five-step checklist to run through when meeting with God. This can be described and explained using the acronym: **S. T. A. N. D.**

Step 1: Surrender yourselves unto God

Repent and confess of any sin before God. Allow Him to refine and purify your heart and mind. Prepare your heart to meet with Him. Acknowledge and submit to Him as the Almighty God.

Step 2: "Top up" your life with the presence and power of the Holy Spirit

Ask Him to fill you afresh with the Holy Spirit because we cannot pray without the Holy Spirit. Open your heart for renewal and restoration so that you can experience revival.

Step 3: Arm yourself against the enemy

Put on the full armour of God to fight the good fight of faith. Position yourself in heavenly places, seated with Christ and destined for victory.

Step 4: Nullify/neutralise your own thoughts and desires and quiet your soul

Surrender the things you want to pray about - your desires and requests. This means you prepare your heart for whatever God desires. Honour Him above all. Wait in silent expectancy and be dead to your own expectations.

Step 5: Delight yourself in God

Approach Him in faith of the finished work of the cross.

Praise Him for who He is and choose to serve and follow Him as your delight and first love. Remain in faith while you wait on Him with praise and thanksgiving.

This is the inheritance of the saints. To meet with the God Almighty is a privilege through Jesus Christ and a means to become empowered daily to walk with Him.

And I heard a loud voice in heaven, saying, "Now the salvation and the power and the kingdom of our God and the authority of his Christ have come, for the accuser of our brothers has been thrown down, who accuses them day and night before our God. And they have conquered him by the blood of the Lamb and by the word of their testimony, for they loved not their lives even unto death. Revelation 12:10-11

Let's Pray!

APPLICATION

Write down three things you have learned from this Chapter:

____

____

____

____

____

Which truths have you learned that you will commit to apply in your devotion to God:

____

____

____

____

____

How and in what way will you apply this truth in your daily devotion?

____

____

____

____

____

Prayer:
Father God, help me to develop a discipline of prayer. Jesus, teach me to pray like You prayed through the power of the Holy Spirit. Amen.

Chapter 7

Our Father in Heaven,
Hallowed be Your Name

GOD OUR FATHER

When a person is born again, they become a child of God. Now they have a new Father, and they are in a new relationship with God, a covenant relationship through Jesus. Because of the complete work of the cross they can call on God as their ABBA (intimate) Father (Isaiah 63:16; 64:8). The blood of Jesus Christ was how God adopted us into His family, and because of the virtue of Jesus' blood a new covenant with new terms was established between man and "Our Father who art in Heaven."

> *And because you are sons, God has sent the Spirit of his Son into our hearts, crying, "Abba! Father!" So you are no longer a slave, but a son, and if a son, then an heir through God. Galatians 4:6*

Fatherhood is only possible and traceable in two ways, through biological birth or adoption. In this relationally broken world we are living in, it's very rare to find healthy family units. Only through the grace and wisdom of God, are households built and sanctified for His glory. When fatherhood is rejected, families are abandoned. The first thing our heavenly Father wants us to experience in this new covenant is Him as the perfect Father in His family.

> *You therefore must be perfect, as your heavenly Father is perfect.*
> *Matthew 5:48*

> *Every good gift and every perfect gift is from above, coming down from the Father of lights, with whom there is no variation or shadow due to change. Of his own will he brought us forth by the word of truth, that we should be a kind of first-fruits of his creatures. James 1:17-18*

Today all over the world, one of the biggest social issues we face is fatherlessness. Separation and divorce are at the core of our society today and children and healthy families are no longer a priority. God is not surprised however by this lack because He is perfect, and He demonstrated His heart to a fatherless people by sending Jesus His Son to us.

Through the offering of His Son, He invited all people back into a perfect relationship with Him. When fathers return to their calling, God will bring about restoration. He longs to restore all generations of mankind to His original plan.

> *God said to Moses, "I AM WHO I AM." And he said, "Say this to the people of Israel: 'I AM has sent me to you.'" God also said to Moses, "Say this to the people of Israel: 'The LORD, the God of your fathers, the God of Abraham, the God of Isaac, and the God of Jacob, has sent me to you.' This is my name forever, and thus I am to be remembered throughout all generations. Exodus 3:14-15*

We are not just born and destined to live our lives according to the plans of our biological parents, but we are further called to allow our heavenly Father to take His appropriate place in our lives as the true Father of all fathers, the God of all the generations in the world.

> *But to all who did receive him, who believed in his name, he gave the right to become children of God, who were born, not of blood nor of the will of the flesh nor of the will of man, but of God. John 1:12-13*

This is our true lineage, children of the living God. He adopted us as His own, redeemed us by His blood, treated us as His beloved and sealed our relationship with an everlasting covenant. He forgave us our trespasses according to the riches of His grace.

> *Blessed be the God and Father of our Lord Jesus Christ, who has blessed us in Christ with every spiritual blessing in the heavenly places, even as he chose us in him before the foundation of the world, that we should be holy and blameless before him. In love he predestined us for adoption to himself as sons through Jesus Christ, according to the purpose of his will, to the praise of his glorious grace, with which he has blessed us in the Beloved. In him we have redemption through his blood, the forgiveness of our trespasses, according to the riches of his grace, which he lavished upon us, in all wisdom and insight making known to us the mystery of his will, according to his purpose, which he set forth in Christ as a plan for the fullness of time, to unite all things in him, things in heaven and things on earth. Ephesians 1:3-10*

THE SEVEN-FOLD PROMISE OF THE NEW COVENANT[8]

Right through the Bible, we see that freedom and reconciliation were achieved through the offering of blood and the cutting of covenants. God's people in the Old Testament had certain covenantal benefits over any outsiders. God inscribed these blessings in His covenantal names while dealing with Israel in the Old Testament. These blessings were confirmed through the gracious death of His Son and the benefits were carried over through Jesus into the new covenant. We as children of the Father by virtue of the blood of Jesus Christ have access to these seven-fold blessings because of the new covenant:

1. Forgiveness of sin and deliverance from its dominion over our lives.

2. Access to God and the fullness of the indwelling Holy Spirit within us.

3. The promise of health, healing and wholeness of spirit, soul and body.

4. Freedom from the curse of the Law and in Christ, destined for success.

5. Freedom from anxiety and the fear of death and hell.

6. Victory over Satan and the forces of darkness.

7. Chosen by God to fulfil the commission and mandate of Christ.

Dr. Larry Lea said it as follows:

"The blood has cut off the past, dealt with the present and will secure us for the future."

God gave us a wonderful promise concerning His covenant with our forefathers. The prerequisite for getting what He promised is to turn to Him in repentance. This gives us the advantage of praying from the platform of our covenant with Him.

> *But if they confess their iniquity and the iniquity of their fathers in their treachery that they committed against me, and also in walking contrary to me, so that I walked contrary to them and brought them into the land of their enemies—if then their uncircumcised heart is humbled and they make amends for their iniquity, then I will remember my covenant with Jacob, and I will remember my covenant with Isaac and my covenant with Abraham, and I will remember the land. Leviticus 26:40-42*

---

8 A substantial amount of context in this part were taken from the resources of Dr. Larry Lea

Let's delve deeper into the comparison of these blessings towards the covenant names of God and how it helps us in our prayer time. We will align ten names of God with the seven covenantal blessings we receive through Jesus Christ. We praise Him for what He has done for us through the Gospel, and we call upon His name in prayer.

HALLOWED BE YOUR NAME

Revelation knowledge of our God and Father to whom we pray is our starting point. This is revealed through His covenantal names. The benefits that we have acquired through Him and His corresponding names, are given to us for approaching His throne in prayer. We come into His presence with thanksgiving that we can call Him Father by virtue of the blood of Jesus. We hallow His names which points to their fulfilment in the person and the work of the Lord Jesus Christ.

The names **Jehovah** (YHWH) and **Adoniah** which means Lord and Master were used by God's people to confirm their eternal covenant with Him. More of the revelation of who He is will be established in our lives as we daily call on these names.

Benefit #1: Forgiveness of sin and deliverance from its dominion.

The first compound name of God which points towards His dealings with our sin is **Jehovah-Tsidkenu**, meaning *"Jehovah our righteousness."* It is very significant that we start our time of prayer with this name of God. Because the question was raised; how can a sinful man be acquitted of his unrighteousness and become righteous before God? For God is righteous (Psalm 97:2) and man is evil (Jeremiah 17:9), and a righteous God cannot overlook man's unrighteousness (Exodus 23:7, Romans 6:23), as no man is innocent.

Mankind was found in a place of guilt and condemnation before God, because of Adam's sin. So how can a sinful man be acquitted of his unrighteousness and become righteous before God? The only way of redemption and right standing before God, was not to be found in their efforts of religious duties, but only in a righteousness coming from God. For all our works and efforts are like filthy rags before Him. Remember that **Jehovah-Tsidkenu** is a covenant name of an eternal God and, even today, we cannot save ourselves, but we need a Saviour. This replacement was prophesied by Jeremiah.

Behold, the days are coming, declares the LORD, when I will raise up for David a righteous Branch, and he shall reign as king and deal wisely, and shall execute justice and righteousness in the land. Jeremiah 23:5

We find the answer to this difficulty in the following verses from Isaiah 64.

We have all become like one who is unclean, and all our righteous deeds are like a polluted garment. We all fade like a leaf, and our iniquities, like the wind, take us away. There is no one who calls upon your name, who rouses himself to take hold of you; for you have hidden your face from us, and have made us melt in the hand of our iniquities. But now, O LORD, you are our Father; we are the clay, and you are our potter; we are all the work of your hand. Isaiah 64:6-8

We see that mankind could not keep their covenant with God, but God made a way for mankind to return to Him in righteousness by sending His Son Jesus. Isaiah then declares that we have a Father, who can remould us into a likeness of His righteousness through the sacrifice of His Son.

Now we stand in this new covenant with God. His righteousness is a free gift to us and it restores us back into a relationship with God, the same kind of relationship as Adam initially had with Him.

For our sake he made him to be sin who knew no sin, so that in him we might become the righteousness of God. 2 Corinthians 5:21

For, being ignorant of the righteousness of God, and seeking to establish their own, they did not submit to God's righteousness. For Christ is the end of the law for righteousness to everyone who believes. Romans 10:3-4

The provision of this righteousness was made in Jesus Christ who was substituted by God for us. (2 Corinthians 5:21, 1 Peter 3:18). Jesus is our **Jehovah-Tsidkenu**, our righteousness.

For if, because of one man's trespass, death reigned through that one man, much more will those who receive the abundance of grace and the free gift of righteousness reign in life through the one man Jesus Christ. Therefore, as one trespass led to condemnation for all men, so one act of righteousness leads to justification and life for all men. Romans 5:17-18

Another compound name of God for the dealings of our sin was **Jehovah-M'kaddesh**, which means *"Jehovah who sanctifies."* This name also refers to being set apart for service. God is the Sanctifier of His people through Jesus' blood, and through the Holy Spirit, we are empowered to live holy lives. (1 Corinthians 6:11, 1 Thessalonians 4:3-4; 5:23)

As we adore and call on these names, **Jehovah-Tsidkeno** and **Jehovah-M'kaddesh**, we thank Him for the forgiveness of our sins and His power that helps us to overcome sin and its dominion. We praise God our Father that we are declared righteous through Jesus Christ and that He continually sanctifies us.

Benefit #2: Access to God and the fullness of the indwelling Holy Spirit within us.

Because God is our Father, the second benefit we enjoy in the new covenant is the fullness of His Spirit. The compound name, **Jehovah-Shalom**, means *"Jehovah our peace"* representing wholeness and harmony with God, and contentment and satisfaction in life for man. Christ's atonement is the basis of our peace with God.

> *For in him all the fullness of God was pleased to dwell, and through him to reconcile to himself all things, whether on earth or in heaven, making peace by the blood of his cross. And you, who once were alienated and hostile in mind, doing evil deeds, he has now reconciled in his body of flesh by his death, in order to present you holy and blameless and above reproach before him. Colossians 1:19-22*

By His atoning blood Jesus broke down the barrier that separated us from God. The veil was torn in two, opening the way for us in the holy of holies - the very presence of God.

> *Therefore, brothers, since we have confidence to enter the holy places by the blood of Jesus, by the new and living way that he opened for us through the curtain, that is, through his flesh, and since we have a great priest over the house of God, let us draw near with a true heart in full assurance of faith, with our hearts sprinkled clean from an evil conscience and our bodies washed with pure water. Hebrews 10:19-22*

Another covenantal name of God, **Jehovah-Shammah,** means *"Jehovah is there"* and points towards the holy God who dwells in the midst of His people. We are His living temples; our sins are forgiven, and we can be filled with the presence of the Holy Spirit.

Now may the God of peace himself sanctify you completely, and may your whole spirit and soul and body be kept blameless at the coming of our Lord Jesus Christ. 1 Thessalonians 5:23

Benefit #3: The promise of health, healing and wholeness of spirit, soul, and body.

The third benefit we enjoy in the new covenant is health and healing. The name of God, **Jehovah-Rapha**, means *"Jehovah heals"*. The word *"rophe"* means to restore, cure, and heal, not only in the physical sense but also in the spiritual, emotional, and moral sense.

We put our faith in the finished work of the cross and thank our Father that we are healed by the stripes of Jesus. Hallow the name of **Jehovah-Rapha**, He is our healer.

> *He himself bore our sins in his body on the tree, that we might die to sin and live to righteousness. By his wounds you have been healed. 1 Peter 2:24*

God gave us many promises about healing in His Word, and Jesus confirmed the Father's heart by healing many people while He was on earth. We can, therefore, stand on His Word and claim our healing by calling on the name of **Jehovah-Rapha**.

> *He sent out his word and healed them, and delivered them from their destruction. Psalm 107:20*

Benefit #4: Freedom from the curse of the Law and in Christ, destined for success.

The fourth benefit of the new covenant in Jesus Christ is freedom from the curse of the Law. All men have sinned and have fallen short of the glory of God, (Rom 3:23) therefore, they were cursed. Nobody has ever fulfilled the requirements of the Law for it relies on good works. Access to God was allowed based on performance and not on faith.

> *For all who rely on works of the law are under a curse; for it is written, "Cursed be everyone who does not abide by all things written in the Book of the Law, and do them." Now it is evident that no one is justified before God by the law, for "The righteous shall live by faith." Galatians 3:10-11*

However, through the blood of Jesus Christ we were redeemed from this curse and destined for success. There is now no condemnation for those who are in Christ.

> *Christ redeemed us from the curse of the law by becoming a curse or us— for it is written, "Cursed is everyone who is hanged on a tree"— so that in Christ Jesus the blessing of Abraham might come to the Gentiles, so that we might receive the promised Spirit through faith. Galatians 3:13-14*

When the soldiers created a crown of thorns and put it on Christ's head, they did not realize the significance of their actions. Thorns symbolize the curse (Gen 3:17-18). In this way, Jesus bore the curse in our place that we might inherit the blessings of Abraham.

Another name of God, **Jehovah-Jireh**, means *"Jehovah's provision shall be seen"* is related to this blessing. On the cross, Jesus took the curse of our failures, inferiority and insufficiency and became our **Jehovah-Jireh**. God asked Abraham to offer his son on a mountain in Moriah. Isaac represented the fulfilment of the promises and blessings of God in Abraham's life. He obeyed God and rose early in the morning to go and prepare Isaac as an offering of worship unto God. We know that this was not just something Abraham did, but also a prophetic reference to Jesus who was crucified in our place. On that day God provided a ram as a substitute for Isaac and Abraham called the place "The LORD will provide."

> *And Abraham lifted up his eyes and looked, and behold, behind him was a ram, caught in a thicket by his horns. And Abraham went and took the ram and offered it up as a burnt offering instead of his son. So Abraham called the name of that place, "The LORD will provide"; as it is said to this day, "On the mount of the LORD it shall be provided." And the angel of the LORD called to Abraham a second time from heaven and said, "By myself I have sworn, declares the LORD, because you have done this and have not withheld your son, your only son, I will surely bless you, and I will surely multiply your offspring as the stars of heaven and as the sand that is on the seashore. And your offspring shall possess the gate of his enemies, and in your offspring shall all the nations of the earth be blessed, because you have obeyed my voice." Genesis 22:13-18*

In the same way Jesus was sacrificed as a substitute for us and because of the Lamb of God we can live free from the curse of sin. God sees our needs beforehand and provides for them. His name Jehovah-Jireh is a revelation of His willingness and ability to meet every need of His people.

Benefit #5: Freedom from anxiety and the fear of death and hell.

The fifth benefit we enjoy in our new covenant is freedom from anxiety and the fear of death and hell. The compound name of God, **Jehovah-Nissi**, means *"Jehovah my banner"* was given to Moses. A banner to the Jews was a sign of deliverance and salvation, a signal to God's people to run towards Him, and it represented His cause, and His battle.

> *And Moses built an altar and called the name of it, The LORD Is My Banner, saying, "A hand upon the throne of the LORD! The LORD will have war with Amalek from generation to generation." Exodus 17:15-16*

Isaiah prophesied that a root would come from the stem of Jesse and would stand as a signal for the people. This stem is Jesus Christ, He is the banner of our redemption and warfare. He has abolished death and has brought life and immortality to light through the gospel.

> *In that day the root of Jesse, who shall stand as a signal for the peoples—of him shall the nations inquire, and his resting place shall be glorious. Isaiah 11:10*

He gives us victory and makes us conquerors (Rom 8:31, 37). Praise Him for eternal life and His life that works in and through us to quicken our mortal bodies. (John 10:27-28)

> *But thanks be to God, who gives us the victory through our Lord Jesus Christ. 1 Corinthians 15:57*

> *If the Spirit of him who raised Jesus from the dead dwells in you, he who raised Christ Jesus from the dead will also give life to your mortal bodies through his Spirit who dwells in you. Romans 8:11*

Another name of God, **Jehovah-Rohi,** means *"Jehovah my shepherd"* is related to this blessing. The primary word of *"rohi"* is to feed and lead to pasture, as a shepherd does with his flock. Jesus is the good Shepherd (John 10:11) and we don't have to fear or live with anxiety. He is watching over us with love and care. He knows of every need, and we can call on Him for His care.

Rejoice in the Lord always; again I will say, rejoice. Let your reasonableness be known to everyone. The Lord is at hand; do not be anxious about anything, but in everything by prayer and supplication with thanksgiving let your requests be made known to God. And the peace of God, which surpasses all understanding, will guard your hearts and your minds in Christ Jesus. Philippians 4:4-7

Benefit #6: Victory over Satan and the forces of darkness.

The sixth benefit we have through Jesus in the new covenant is complete victory over Satan and the forces of darkness. Yes, we are more than conquerors through Christ Jesus.

The sting of death is sin, and the power of sin is the law. But thanks be to God, who gives us the victory through our Lord Jesus Christ.
1 Corinthians 15:56-57

No, in all these things we are more than conquerors through him who loved us. For I am sure that neither death nor life, nor angels nor rulers, nor things present nor things to come, nor powers, nor height nor depth, nor anything else in all creation, will be able to separate us from the love of God in Christ Jesus our Lord. Romans 8:37-39

The part *"from the love of God in Christ Jesus our Lord,"* points us directly back to the victory on the cross over evil forces and the power of Satan. We read in the Old Testament of God as *"the God of hosts"* (Isaiah 1:9, 1 Samuel 1:3). Hannah the mother of Samuel could not have children and vowed in her prayer to the *"God of hosts"* in the temple as she worshiped Him.

And she vowed a vow and said, "O LORD of hosts, if you will indeed look on the affliction of your servant and remember me and not forget your servant, but will give to your servant a son, then I will give him to the LORD all the days of his life, and no razor shall touch his head." As she continued praying before the LORD, Eli observed her mouth. Hannah was speaking in her heart; only her lips moved, and her voice was not heard.
1 Samuel 1:11-13

The name of God, **Jehovah-Tsaba**, means *"the God of the armies"* and is used in these verses. David said the following, when he had to fight against Goliath: "You come to me with a sword and with a spear and with a javelin, *but I come to you in the name of the LORD of hosts, the God of the armies of Israel."*

Moses had a similar experience when they were leaving Egypt. At first God promised to Moses the victory and in the end, he led God's people out victoriously.

> *And Moses said to the people, "Fear not, stand firm, and see the salvation of the LORD, which he will work for you today. For the Egyptians whom you see today, you shall never see again. The LORD will fight for you, and you have only to be silent." Exodus 14:13-14*

Is God fighting for us? We all know that Jesus overcame the power of sin and death, but God keeps on fighting for us. For we are still in this continuous battle raging in the world and need to stand firm against the schemes and the powers of darkness, holding onto the promises of victory through our Lord Jesus Christ, and fighting the good fight of our faith. (1 Timothy 6:12)

> *Finally, be strong in the Lord and in the strength of his might. Put on the whole armor of God, that you may be able to stand against the schemes of the devil. For we do not wrestle against flesh and blood, but against the rulers, against the authorities, against the cosmic powers over this present darkness, against the spiritual forces of evil in the heavenly places. Therefore take up the whole armor of God, that you may be able to withstand in the evil day, and having done all, to stand firm. Ephesians 6:10-13*

> *The God of peace will soon crush Satan under your feet. The grace of our Lord Jesus Christ be with you. Romans 16:20*

The name of God, **Jehovah-Tsuri**, means *"The Lord my Rock"*, and it should give us enough security and stability to stand firm in what He has promised in His Word. Jesus said to His disciples that He will build His church upon the rock, referring to Himself, the Christ as the rock. Calling upon **Jehovah-Tsuri** will establish Christ as the firm foundation in our lives.

Benefit #7: Chosen by God to fulfil the mandate and commission of Christ.

The Bible tells us that God loved this world so much that He sent His one and only Son Jesus, for whoever believes in him should not perish but have eternal life. He was sent not to condemn mankind but to save them. Jesus came to seek and save those who were lost, lost eternally, and lost for the kingdom of God on earth. (John 3:16-18; Luke 19:10)

The Word of God continues by saying;

"Whoever believes in the Son has eternal life; whoever does not obey the Son shall not see life, but the wrath of God remains on him" John 3:36

John the Baptist testified about Jesus as the *"Lamb of God"* and said to his disciples that a person cannot receive anything unless it is given to him from heaven. John admitted to his followers that he is not the Christ, but a friend of the bridegroom. He confessed that He, Jesus, who came from heaven is above all things. Angels also prophesied about Jesus to His biological parents as follows:

She will bear a son, and you shall call his name Jesus, for he will save his people from their sins." All this took place to fulfil what the Lord had spoken by the prophet: "Behold, the virgin shall conceive and bear a son, and they shall call his name Immanuel" (which means, God with us). Matthew 1:21-23

The name of God, **Immanuel**, means *"God with us"* and was given to Jesus and in Him all the fullness of our heavenly Father dwells.

For in him all the fullness of God was pleased to dwell, and through him to reconcile to himself all things, whether on earth or in heaven, making peace by the blood of his cross. Colossians 1:19-20

The New Testament name **Immanuel** corresponds well with the Old Testament name **Lord God** (YHWH Elohim). The one who creates, who rules overall and sustains everything. As the Redeemer of mankind, He achieved reconciliation for all people and reconciled us back to the Father. He gave us the ministry of reconciliation and He appointed us as ambassadors for Him.

All this is from God, who through Christ reconciled us to himself and gave us the ministry of reconciliation; that is, in Christ God was reconciling the world to himself, not counting their trespasses against them, and entrusting to us the message of reconciliation. Therefore, we are ambassadors for Christ, God making his appeal through us. We implore you on behalf of Christ, be reconciled to God. 2 Corinthians 5:18-20

After His resurrection from the dead, Jesus commanded His disciples to go and preach the Gospel to all people and proclaim His name in all the nations of the world. He promised to be with us, always, to the end of the age.

And behold, I am with you always, to the end of the age. Matthew 28:20

He is indeed our **Immanuel**, God with us, forever!

The name of God, **Jehovah-Shammah**, *"The Lord is there"* or *"The presence of the Lord is with us"* will continually encourage us to live our lives to fulfill His mandate on earth. We must be reminded daily that we are not operating in our own strength but in His power and that He promised to be with us, forever!

As we meditate upon these names of God and in prayer call upon Him for our inner strength and empowerment, we will do greater things for Him and so fulfil His mandate and commission on earth.

Let's Pray!

APPLICATION

Write down three things you have learned from this Chapter:

____

____

____

____

Which truths have you learned that you will commit to apply in your devotion to God:

____

____

____

____

How and in what way will you apply this truth in your daily devotion?

____

____

____

____

Prayer:
Thank you God, that you are my heavenly Father. I appreciate the covenant that I have with You through the blood of Jesus Christ. I want to walk closely with You and to experience the power of this covenant in my life. Teach me more about the power of Your Name and who You are. Thank you for all the wonderful promises we have in Your Word. Amen.

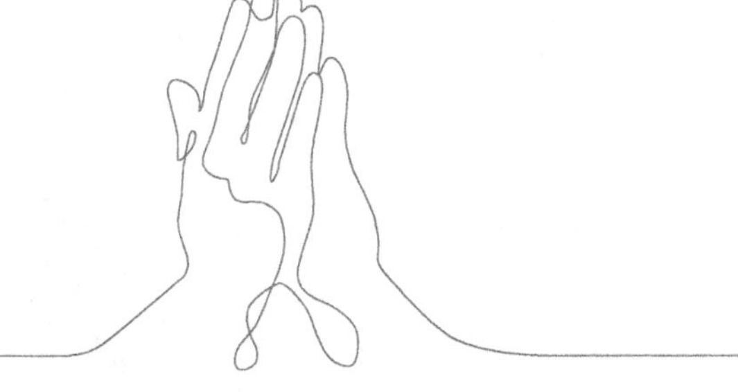

Chapter 8

Your Kingdom come,
Your Will be done

YOUR KINGDOM COME, YOUR WILL BE DONE

This chapter involves asking, seeking, and knocking at the door of heaven to petition for the attention of YHWH Elohim, our creator LORD God to intervene on earth. In our daily prayer we request for the rule and reign of God to inhabit our lives, the lives of our families and those we have relationships with, as well as the communities and nations that we are exposed to. In essence, we seek the dominion of the King of kings and Lord of lords throughout the earth. This is where we pray for God to show us what He desires us to prioritise in our lives. Are we willing to submit to God's will in this regard?

It is very important to notice that this part of the Lord's prayer: *"Your kingdom come, your will be done"*, is written in the active form of the original text and not in the passive form, which means we should actively command God's kingdom and will to be done. God's kingdom and His will holds everything together in our lives and in this world. When the children of God start to seek God's kingdom, denying their own selfish will and laying down their lives; that is when God's kingdom will come. Jesus said:

Therefore do not be anxious, saying, 'What shall we eat?' or 'What shall we drink?' or 'What shall we wear?' For the Gentiles seek after all these things, and your heavenly Father knows that you need them all. But seek first the kingdom of God and his righteousness, and all these things will be added to you. Matthew 6:31-33

And in another place, He said:

But not a hair of your head will perish. Luke 18:21

The Psalmist wrote:

When I look at your heavens, the work of your fingers, the moon and the stars, which you have set in place, what is man that you are mindful of him, and the son of man that you care for him? Yet you have made him a little lower than the heavenly beings and crowned him with glory and honor. You have given him dominion over the works of your hands; you have put all things under his feet. Psalm 8:3-6

Setting and maintaining priorities is a common problem especially when it comes to spiritual discipline. At many points in our lives, we all have attempted to change our lifestyle to one of deeper devotion to God. The most liberating news about God's kingdom is that it comes to us, with the only requirement being to surrender with a repentant heart. (Matthew 3:2) In fact, according to the gospel of Luke, God's kingdom is in our midst.

The kingdom of God is not coming in ways that can be observed, nor will they say, 'Look, here it is!' or 'There!' for behold, the kingdom of God is in the midst of you.   Luke 17:20-21

We can only do our part and trust the Lord to renew His priorities in our hearts through the power of the Holy Spirit. Prayer is a way of achieving this goal.

Everything valuable carries a price, and this holds true for the kingdom of God. Jesus mentioned in His sermon on the mount, one of the most important requirements for receiving God's kingdom.

Blessed are the poor in spirit, for theirs is the kingdom of heaven. Matthew 5:3

What is the Kingdom of God?

The kingdom of heaven is like the hidden treasure after which wise men sought, the fine pearls merchants desired, and the good seed the sower sowed. It is like the small grain of mustard-seed that grew to become a tree for birds to make their nests. It's like a net thrown into the sea gathering all kinds of fish, and like the leaven women used for bread.

God's kingdom is open to the masters of households, scribes, and little children. Anyone can have access to the Kingdom of heaven through submission to God's will. It's simple but costly. Although simple, it has a major impact on our lives if we accept it, and only those that humble themselves like little children will be the greatest within the kingdom. It's immeasurable, indescribable, difficult to explain, and impossible to attain without the rulership of the King of heaven.

During the times of the New Testament, the people were under the rule and reign of the Roman empire. It was difficult to stand up against the Roman law and live according to all the Christian values. Persecution was at the door of those who followed Jesus. The apostle Paul provided some insight on the Roman church by defining the kingdom of God.

For the kingdom of God is not a matter of eating and drinking but of righteousness and peace and joy in the Holy Spirit. Whoever thus serves Christ is acceptable to God and approved by men. So then let us pursue what makes for peace and for mutual upbuilding. Romans 14:17-19

We are in very similar situations today and therefore it is relevant and important for us to pray for the kingdom of God to come. We pray for His righteousness, His peace, and His joy to come on earth. God's kingdom has a king - Jesus. When we pray *"your kingdom come"* and *"your will be done"*; we are asking for His Lordship over our lives and the spheres of life in which we operate and navigate. Paul continues to describe the kingdom of God to the Corinthian church as the *"power of God."* (1 Corinthians 4:20) This power produces God's righteousness, peace, and joy in our hearts when we pray, *"let Your kingdom come, let your will be done!"*

God's kingdom is an everlasting kingdom that will stand eternally. His kingdom will shatter all other kingdoms, and therefore it is such a privilege for the children of God to pray for the kingdom of God to come.

And in the days of those kings the God of heaven will set up a kingdom that shall never be destroyed, nor shall the kingdom be left to another people. It shall break in pieces all these kingdoms and bring them to an end, and it shall stand forever. Daniel 2:44

What is the will of God?

God's will is clearly defined in the Bible and when we pray according to scripture we will hardly miss it. Because when we pray according to the Word, which is His will, we also establish His kingdom in our lives. God's will and kingdom cannot be separated from one another.

We will not be able to pray effectively for His will to come without surrendering our will. By presenting our bodies to God as His temple, we align ourselves and our priorities to His. Obedience will always come after surrender, and it is the only way that we will experience Godly outcomes to our prayers. Praying for His will to come will help us to reject the ungodly and be renewed to discern God's kingdom and will. When we pray for God's will to come, we're asking and allowing God in honesty to make the next call.

I appeal to you therefore, brothers, by the mercies of God, to present your bodies as a living sacrifice, holy and acceptable to God, which is your spiritual worship. Do not be conformed to this world, but be transformed by the renewal of your mind, that by testing you may discern what is the will of God, what is good and acceptable and perfect. Romans 12:1-2

It is possible to live according to God's will. It is a standard of living and demands a surrendered lifestyle of worship. All believers should desire to follow God's will daily. The blessing of living this kind of life is that He listens to those when they call to Him in prayer.

We know that God does not listen to sinners, but if anyone is a worshiper of God and does his will, God listens to him. John 9:31

For whoever does the will of God, he is my brother and sister and mother." Mark 3:35

Following the will of God everyday will establish within us a sensitivity for His approval against those of men, wanting to please Him above anything else. As mature disciples, we will live in the power of His Spirit with sincere hearts.

Bondservants, obey your earthly masters with fear and trembling, with a sincere heart, as you would Christ, not by the way of eye-service, as people-pleasers, but as bondservants of Christ, doing the will of God from the heart, rendering service with a good will as to the Lord and not to man. Ephesians 6:5-7

The main aim of God's will in anyone's life is holiness. Complete dedication in acting out and following His desires and purposes for them. Free from lustful immorality and greedy passions, pure and set apart for His service.

For this is the will of God, your sanctification: that you abstain from sexual immorality; that each one of you know how to control his own body in holiness and honor, not in the passion of lust like the Gentiles who do not know God; that no one transgress and wrong his brother in this matter, because the Lord is an avenger in all these things, as we told you beforehand and solemnly warned you. For God has not called us for impurity, but in holiness. 1 Thessalonians 4:3-7

As obedient children, do not be conformed to the passions of your former ignorance, but as he who called you is holy, you also be holy in all your conduct, since it is written, "You shall be holy, for I am holy." 1 Peter 1:14-16

How Can We Know the Will of God?

We can know the will of God by the promises in His Word. We need to settle in our hearts the truth that God's Word is the foundation of His will. The Bible was given to us for the specific purpose of revealing to us the will of God, and when we find that anything is promised in the Word of God, we know that that is His will, for He has said so in so many words. In the same manner, it is very important to interpret the Word of God correctly.

When we who believe in the name of the Son of God go to God and ask Him for anything that is promised in His Word, we can know with absolute certainty that God has heard our prayer and that the thing that we have asked of God is granted. We do not have to feel it; God says so, and that is enough. When you have a definite promise in God's Word, you do not need to put any "ifs" before it. All the promises of God are yes and amen in Christ Jesus." [9]

> *For all the promises of God find their Yes in him. That is why it is through him that we utter our Amen to God for his glory. 2 Corinthians 1:20*

On earth as it is in heaven

None of us knows what heaven is like. Therefore, we don't always specifically know what praying for the kingdom of heaven looks like. But Jesus knows, He is the king of heaven and earth and He said we should pray like this. Every believer can be involved in achieving this, for we all can pray and should endure in this practice of continually reminding God about His promises given in His Word.

> *For you have need of endurance, so that when you have done the will of God you may receive what is promised. Hebrew 10:36*

> *Watch and pray that you may not enter into temptation. The spirit indeed is willing, but the flesh is weak. Matthew 26:41.*

It is through prayer that the kingdom and will of God should be established, first in us and secondly through us. This is a spiritual battle, a war in the heavenlies and sometimes a travail in tears for the followers of Christ. It is a demonstration of His power here on earth.

---

9   Torrey, Reuben A. The Power of Prayer and the Prayer of Power

We're going to focus while praying for His kingdom and will to come in four major areas:

1. Our own lives and households.

2. Our churches and all the different ministries.

3. Our relatives, friends, communities, and workplaces.

4. Our nation, communities, and the harvest fields of the world.

Unite in prayer

When we as believers unite regularly in our efforts and prayer, this will result in God's kingdom and will be done in private and public spaces, and revival will be the natural consequence. While these first disciples in the book of Acts prayed together, heaven came down and the church was established and strengthened through prayer:

- The Holy Spirit was poured out on all people (Acts 2).

- The lame was healed (Acts 3).

- The number of disciples increased (Acts 2 & 6).

- Devotion to God increased (Acts 2 & 6).

- New vision and revelation came to the church (Acts 10 & 11).

- Prisoners were released (Acts 12 & 16).

- New church plants were started, and leaders were sent on missions (Acts 13 & 24).

- Boldness, signs and miracles increased, and many were filled with the Spirit (Acts 4).

- Influential people repented and turned to God (Acts 8 & 9).

Prayer is the key to unlock heaven and releases the power of God on earth. Prevailing through prayer is one way in which the kingdom and will of God can come to us. As children of God, we have the privilege of asking, seeking, and knocking at the door of heaven to petition for the attention of our Father to intervene on earth.

Let's Pray!

APPLICATION

Write down three things you have learned from this Chapter:

____

____

____

____

Which truths have you learned that you will commit to apply in your devotion to God:

____

____

____

____

How and in what way will you apply this truth in your daily devotion?

____

____

____

____

Prayer:
Father, let Your Kingdom come and Your will to be done in my life, family, community, church and nation. Release your power over us and help us to unite to do Your will. Show me what to do to make it happen, in the name of Jesus. Amen.

Chapter 9

Give us this day our daily bread

GIVE US THIS DAY OUR DAILY BREAD

It is a blessing to be part of God's kingdom; to be called children of the most high God; adopting our identity as heirs of the Almighty and walking in the assurance of a loving Father. As previously mentioned, one of God's covenant names is **Jehovah Rohi**, our Shepherd who cares for us. The God we serve is so versatile and can't be described with one name only.

We have also discussed a bit about the name **Jehovah Jireh**, which points more to the Father who provided a Lamb as a substitute for our sin. He gave us eternal life and that is worth more than our daily bread or the fulfilment of our physical needs.

Another aspect of the name **Jehovah Jireh** means that *"He will show us His provision"* in our lives. When we obey God, it opens a door for His provision in our lives. If we look at the example of Abraham, God called him to sacrifice his son Isaac and showed him the fastened ram, but only after three days of going up the mountain. Abraham and Isaac carried the wood and fire for the offering was a human sacrifice. In the same way, we might not see or find God's provision immediately and sometimes we should wait upon him and trust that he will provide.

Obeying His voice may lead us slowly in the direction of His plan until we come to the final place of offering. Sometimes God will test our endurance and obedience in faith before He brings about a breakthrough. When we call on the Name of **Jehovah Jireh**, we not only praise Him for His eternal provision of an everlasting life, but we also trust Him to cultivate an enduring hope and faith within us to keep on trusting Him for our daily bread. Therefore, we can ask, seek, and knock with full confidence at the door of heaven as **Jehovah Jireh**, our provider will show us something of His provision.

After studying the **'EL'** names of God, we will find three very direct references to a God who is committed to care for our daily needs. The difference between the **'EL'** names and the **'YHWH'** (Jehovah) names is that the **'EL'** names depict God's character while the **'YHWH'** names refer to His covenant. He connected Himself to certain people at specific times in the Old Testament. Let's take a closer look at three of these **'EL'** names of God:

El-Shaddai = The Almighty all sufficient One

Imagine approaching an all-sufficient God for our daily bread, not merely for our monthly needs. This would mean that our intricate plans regarding our tomorrow would be null and void. God doesn't want us to think ahead and try to figure things out with our natural minds. His desire is for us to move from a state of worrying to a state of trusting, fully relying on the God who made the heavens and the earth.

The name *"Shaddai"* means *'breast'* and in the ancient Greek religions we will find a god who is called *'the many breasted one'* and was portrayed as a woman with many breasts. The breast of a mother is the place of feeding for a baby and for some time her milk is all that the baby needs. It is all sufficient and substantial. When we live close to God's heart and feed daily on what He provides us, we will be content with His daily bread.

> *He will tend his flock like a shepherd; he will gather the lambs in his arms; he will carry them in his bosom, and gently lead those that are with young.*
> *Isaiah 40:11*

El-Roi = the God who sees

When Jesus was teaching His disciples to pray, He told them how their Father who sees them when they pray in secret, will reward them, and went on further to say that their Father knows the things they need before they ask Him.

> *But when you pray, go into your room and shut the door and pray to your Father who is in secret. And your Father who sees in secret will reward you.*
> *Matthew 6:6*

The name **El-Roi**[10] was firstly revealed to Hagar when Ismael was at the point of death due to a shortage of water. In secrecy, she cried unto God to provide for her child's basic daily needs, and God saw the faith in her heart and supplied her in her need.

God wants to see the honesty and desire in our hearts for Him before we can witness and access His provision.

---

10 Hagar refers to God as El-Roi, this Name was not directly revealed by God, but God did not correct her.

El-Shammah = The God that hears

Earlier we explained the covenantal name **Jehovah-Shammah**, which was taken from the name **El-Shammah**, which means *'the God who is there' or the 'present God.'* Like a Father being the breadwinner of the household, who is positioned to supply for the needs of his family; in the same we have a God who has positioned Himself on our behalf to be *'present'* for us when we are in need.

> *Before they call I will answer; while they are yet speaking I will hear.*
> *Isaiah 65:24*

> *Then you will call upon me and come and pray to me, and I will hear you. You will seek me and find me, when you seek me with all your heart. Jeremiah 29:12-13*

Throughout the New Testament and especially in the four Gospels we will find many promises of God's provision for His children. This is proof of God's care for us like a shepherd care for his sheep.

> *Therefore I tell you, do not be anxious about your life, what you will eat or what you will drink, nor about your body, what you will put on. Is not life more than food, and the body more than clothing? Look at the birds of the air: they neither sow nor reap nor gather into barns, and yet your heavenly Father feeds them. Are you not of more value than they? Matthew 6:25-26*

> *And my God will supply every need of yours according to his riches in glory in Christ Jesus. Philippians 4:19*

> *Jesus said to them, "I am the bread of life; whoever comes to me shall not hunger, and whoever believes in me shall never thirst. John 6:35*

In this section we are adding to our daily need for spiritual food and intimacy with God, also praying for financial freedom and work satisfaction. Our careers and workplaces are very important to God. He wants to bring complete satisfaction to our lives.

Let's read again very slowly and with meditation through Psalm 23.

The LORD is my shepherd; I shall not want. He makes me lie down in green pastures. He leads me beside still waters. He restores my soul. He leads me in paths of righteousness for his name's sake. Even though I walk through the valley of the shadow of death, I will fear no evil, for you are with me; your rod and your staff, they comfort me. You prepare a table before me in the presence of my enemies; you anoint my head with oil; my cup overflows. Surely goodness and mercy shall follow me all the days of my life, and I shall dwell in the house of the LORD forever. Psalm 23

We should never lose the perspective of the birds of the air or the lilies of the fields. He is our all sufficient One and Provider of all our needs! Call on Him and trust Him every day. A loving Father who promised to care for us more than He does for the birds and lilies of the field.

Let's Pray!

APPLICATION

Write down three things you have learned from this Chapter:

____

____

____

____

____

Which truths have you learned that you will commit to apply in your devotion to God:

____

____

____

____

How and in what way will you apply this truth in your daily devotion?

____

____

____

____

Prayer:
Heavenly Father, thank You that You are our source in life and that You promise to care for Your children. You are the all-sufficient One - the God that provides all our needs. You are all that I need. Amen.

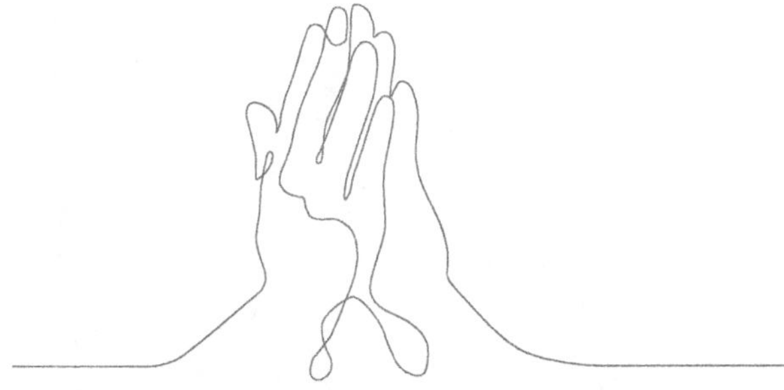

Chapter 10

Forgive us our debts,
as we forgive our debtors

FORGIVE US OUR DEBTS, AS WE FORGIVE OUR DEBTORS

Earlier was mentioned that this section of the prayer will get to the deepest parts of our hearts. This truly reflects the purpose of Jesus' mission. Jesus came and surrendered Himself to make it possible for human beings to pray. Forgiveness is the power of reconciliation between God and all people. It's the application of the Gospel, the implementation of unconditional love and is not possible without putting God's kingdom first in our lives.

Forgiveness is the power of love that brings reconciliation between God and all people. It's the submission unto the kingdom and will of God. It finishes off the outstanding debt and secures restoration to all relationships. It brings complete healing to the spirit, soul and body of man. Forgiveness is possible when we apply truth in our hearts and reconciliation comes when we practice Godly love. It's the end of the reasoning about human errors. Forgiveness is the key that unlocks the love of God in and through us. It's the power that transforms sinners to become saints and the remedy for prodigals to return.

The greatest enemy of forgiveness is pride. Pride is the root to all sin and keeps people away from accepting God's love. Jesus' first words after this teaching on prayer was:

> *For if you forgive others their trespasses, your heavenly Father will also forgive you, but if you do not forgive others their trespasses, neither will your Father forgive your trespasses. Matthew 6:14-15*

The driving force behind unforgiveness is self-righteousness and the mask behind unforgiveness is insecurity and deep-rooted rejection. Unforgiveness is a temporary human arranged reconciliation. A reprieve from the punishment caused by inner debt.

We all must take stock from time to time and apply regular stop-loss measures to warn us against danger. If we don't bind our hearts regularly to God's love and lose ourselves from relational issues, we will not experience God's total freedom. Without forgiveness true freedom is not possible for it is the banner of the saints. The name **Jehovah-Nissi** relates to this freedom. Our banner of victory was truly manifested in the victory of Jesus on the cross. Forgiveness is to stop the inner turmoil, to put aside all claims and to let go of all offences.

Herein I also exercise myself to have a conscience void of offence toward God and men always. Acts 24:16 (ASV)

The reason why forgiveness is so difficult for us is because it is not in our will or power, we need the power of the Holy Spirit to help us. Forgiveness without surrender is not true forgiveness. True forgiveness between people can only happen when they accept God's forgiveness.

Therefore I tell you, her sins, which are many, are forgiven—for she loved much. But he who is forgiven little, loves little." Luke 7:47

Forgiveness is to submit to higher authority and bow the knee to the Lordship of Jesus concerning the matters of our hearts. The practice of forgiving others is not to release them, but to release yourself. Jesus said:

Be merciful, even as your Father is merciful. "Judge not, and you will not be judged; condemn not, and you will not be condemned; forgive, and you will be forgiven; Luke 6:36-37

For with the judgment you pronounce you will be judged, and with the measure you use it will be measured to you. Matthew 7:2

Forgiveness works as a rotating cycle. In the way we forgive others, in the same we will be forgiven. Jesus forgave us all our sins and iniquities unconditionally and in the same we have to forgive. Iniquities are imputed sins, it is those sins that left a scar, those that we struggle to forget. The only way to become free from it is to allow God's forgiveness that works through Jesus Christ to come and forgive us and heal our pain.

So if the Son sets you free, you will be free indeed. John 8:36

Bless the LORD, O my soul, and forget not all his benefits, who forgives all your iniquity ..., He does not deal with us according to our sins, nor repay us according to our iniquities, as far as the east is from the west, so far does he remove our transgressions from us. Psalm 103:2-3,10,12

Unforgiveness is deceptive and many times it is used to retaliate, but no one enjoys any benefit from the practice, and they don't understand the plan of the enemy to keep them bound. Unforgiveness is a hindrance in our relationship with God and prevents our prayers from being answered.

Therefore I tell you, whatever you ask in prayer, believe that you have received it, and it will be yours. And whenever you stand praying, forgive, if you have anything against anyone, so that your Father also who is in heaven may forgive you your trespasses. Mark 11:24-26

Unforgiveness opens the doors of our lives towards Satan to come to steal, kill and destroy. It brings the anger and punishment of the enemy and in the end, we will be delivered under his authority.

And in anger his master delivered him to the jailers, until he should pay all his debt. So also my heavenly Father will do to every one of you, if you do not forgive your brother from your heart." Matthew 18:34-35

Forgiveness is an act of our will, a choice to guard our hearts against offences. When we forgive others, we unlock the jail in our hearts where we've kept them imprisoned. A freedom that belongs to every person who is willing to pray this section of the prayer of Jesus with a true heart.

It is lastly very important for us to walk in true forgiveness towards ourselves, our own mistakes and pain we caused others. Bitterness towards yourself or others releases toxins which many people poison themselves with. To forgive and release is our part; freedom is God's part.

Forgiveness is the power of love that brings reconciliation between God and all people. It's the application of the Gospel, the implementation of unconditional love and is not possible without putting God's kingdom first in our lives. It finishes off the outstanding debt and secures restoration to all relationships.

We should release ourselves and others through regular repentance and forgiveness.

Let's Pray!

APPLICATION

Write down three things you have learned from this Chapter:

____

____

____

____

Which truths have you learned that you will commit to apply in your devotion to God:

____

____

____

____

How and in what way will you apply this truth in your daily devotion?

____

____

____

____

Prayer:
Heavenly Father, thank You for Your forgiveness in my life. Give me a heart that is quick to forgive - a heart that is always free of offence. I pray this in the name of Jesus. Amen.

Chapter 11

And lead us not into temptation
but deliver us from evil

AND LEAD US NOT INTO TEMPTATION BUT DELIVER US FROM EVIL

It would be unwise to enter this part of the prayer not fully aware of our enemies and our daily combat. The Bible warns us very clearly, to be aware of our spiritual battles and not to be oblivious of the forces of darkness.

Finally, be strong in the Lord and in the strength of his might. Put on the whole armor of God, that you may be able to stand against the schemes of the devil. For we do not wrestle against flesh and blood, but against the rulers, against the authorities, against the cosmic powers over this present darkness, against the spiritual forces of evil in the heavenly places. Ephesians 6:10-12

Similarly, we should always stay focused on our position in Christ as born-again children of God. We are seated with Christ in heavenly places. Again, the Word of God gives us guidance and will help us when we pray this section of the prayer.

and raised us up with him and seated us with him in the heavenly places in Christ Jesus, Ephesians 2:6

There is a huge difference in our combat strategy when fighting as victors as opposed to losers. In and through Christ, we have victory, but we still have to fight the good fight of faith. We should never be caught off guard, for the accuser of the children of God is raging against us. It's like playing in a sports game, a team may be far ahead in terms of points and winning, but until the final whistle is blown, the game is not over.

Be sober-minded; be watchful. Your adversary the devil prowls around like a roaring lion, seeking someone to devour. Resist him, firm in your faith, knowing that the same kinds of suffering are being experienced by your brotherhood throughout the world. 1 Peter 5:8-9

And I heard a loud voice in heaven, saying, "Now the salvation and the power and the kingdom of our God and the authority of his Christ have come, for the accuser of our brothers has been thrown down, who accuses them day and night before our God. And they have conquered him by the blood of the Lamb and by the word of their testimony, for they loved not their lives even unto death. Revelation 12:10-11

In the abovementioned text, there are five easy **"to do's"** to live victoriously every day:

1. Be on guard

Almost every household today, from the rich to the poor, have a security plan in place for their safety. Between locks, burglar bars, CCTV cameras, etc. we try to live and keep our valuables safe and secure. This is because we are aware of an enemy who wants to kill, steal, and destroy. Time has shown that outside security systems are not enough, but unless we ourselves are on guard we won't succeed in our efforts.

> *Unless the Lord builds the house those who build it labor in vain. Unless the LORD watches over the city, the watchman stays awake in vain. Psalm 127:1-2*

A phrase from a very popular Christian song says; "*This is how I fight my battles*" - and we should decide in advance how and when we are going to fight our battles. For the battles are real, they come to us disguised in temptation and sometimes it is difficult to discern what the real battle is. We should always be aware of the weakness of our flesh and the blind spots that we allow in our lives.

Therefore, it is recommended to stay alert, to fight daily, to fight as winners with a powerful prayer life that will enable us to defeat the enemy. Satan with his many schemes is planning evil against us. He is a liar and enjoys the destruction of people (John 8:44). He disguises himself as an angel of the light. (2 Corinthians 11:14) Therefore we should be on guard and alert through continuous prayer. Solomon, known as the father of wisdom, writes in Psalm 127 that unless we involve God in our efforts, we do everything in vain. The New Testament supports this same principle.

> *Watch and pray that you may not enter into temptation. The spirit indeed is willing, but the flesh is weak." Matthew 26:41*

> *and give no opportunity to the devil. Ephesians 4:27*

> *Submit yourselves therefore to God. Resist the devil, and he will flee from you. James 4:7*

2. Put on the full armour of God

We put on clothes to protect our bodies against the cold and the elements. We put on masks to prevent getting infected with viruses. Military and security forces have special protective uniforms to enable them to fulfil their job functions. As Christians we also should have daily protection against the enemy. Paul advises the church in Ephesus not to live unaware of the enemies' schemes but to put on the full armour of God. This is how we will be able to stand firm in our daily battles.

Studying Ephesians 6:10-17 will show us six basic principles to put on as the full armour of God. Three of these we have to either fasten or put on, while the other three we have to take up. These are for both offense and defence on the battleground.

- Fastening the waist belt of truth.

- Putting on the breastplate of righteousness.

- As shoes for your feet, putting on the readiness provided by the Gospel of peace.

- Taking up the shield of faith.

- Taking up the helmet of salvation.

- Taking up the sword of the Spirit, which is the word of God.

Arming ourselves is our responsibility. The most important part of the armour of God is not putting it on, but using them correctly, and the Bible is very clear about how to apply it:

> *praying at all times in the Spirit, with all prayer and supplication. To that end, keep alert with all perseverance, making supplication for all the saints. Ephesians 6:18*

Yes, it's through prayer that we can wage war against the enemy. It would be ineffective to wear armour without praying. This is for *'praying at all times with all prayers'*, making supplication for the saints. There are different kinds of prayer but in all of them we should be well armoured.

3. Put on Christ

We should understand what Paul is teaching the church, using an analogy to reveal the truth of spiritual warfare. This is not a fight we should fight in our own efforts, using our own strategies. The only person who already won the battle against Satan is Jesus Christ. Therefore, when we pray this section, we should put on Christ. The Gospel must be central in all our battles. Our victory is not in our strength but in the finished work of Christ. His death and resurrection secured our victory. We can stay up late or fast and pray for days, but unless we focus on Christ in our prayers, we will pray in vain.

> *But put on the Lord Jesus Christ, and make no provision for the flesh, to gratify its desires. Romans 13:14*

Jesus are truly represented in the analogy of the armour we should have and by daily putting it on we are also putting on Christ.

- The belt of truth - Jesus is the Way, the Truth, and the Life (John 14:6).

- The breastplate of righteousness - Jesus is the righteousness of God (2 Corinthians 5:21).

- The shoes of readiness - Jesus is our passion and we preach Him (2 Timothy 4:1-2)

- The shield of faith - Jesus is the author and finisher of our faith (Hebrews 12:1-2)

- The helmet of salvation - Jesus is our salvation (1 Thessalonica 5:9)

- The sword of the Spirit - Jesus is the living Word and two-edged sword (John 1:14; Hebrews 4:12)

Jesus declared to His disciples:

> *I have said these things to you, that in me you may have peace. In the world you will have tribulation. But take heart; I have overcome the world."*
> *John 16:33*

4. Fight every day through prayer

Jesus went with His disciples to a place called Gethsemane right at the end of His ministry during the start of His suffering. There he said to them: *"Sit here, while I go over there and pray."* He became very sorrowful and troubled and said to them: *"My soul is very sorrowful, even to death; remain here, and watch with me."* He went a little farther and He fell on his face and prayed, saying, *"My Father, if it be possible, let this cup pass from me; nevertheless, not as I will, but as you will."* Matthew 26:39

When He returned an hour later, He found the disciples sleeping, and said to them: *"So, could you not watch with me one hour? Watch and pray that you may not enter into temptation. The spirit indeed is willing, but the flesh is weak."* Matthew 26:40-41

Jesus is fully aware of our challenges when it comes to prayer. He is asking us to only pray one hour each day. How long do people work out or exercise to become physically fit and healthy? How long are we willing to pray to be spiritually strong enough to withstand the forces of darkness daily? We will pray more if we are more convicted about the power of prayer. This is how we fight our battles. Daily disciplined prayer will secure us against our enemies.

> *For the weapons of our warfare are not of the flesh but have divine power to destroy strongholds. We destroy arguments and every lofty opinion raised against the knowledge of God, and take every thought captive to obey Christ, being ready to punish every disobedience, when your obedience is complete. 2 Corinthians 10:4-6*

> *But as for you, O man of God, flee these things. Pursue righteousness, godliness, faith, love, steadfastness, gentleness. Fight the good fight of the faith. Take hold of the eternal life to which you were called and about which you made the good confession in the presence of many witnesses. 1 Timothy 6:11-12*

> *I have fought the good fight, I have finished the race, I have kept the faith. 2 Timothy 4:7*

One of the main reasons why people struggle to pray longer is because they don't know how to pray. We should do what Jesus did - disciple people in daily prayer.

5. Building a Hedge of Protection

It is God's desire and will that we should be strong and protected against the forces of darkness. Job and his family were protected, and when Satan wanted to attack him, he had to ask God's permission. Let's read the scriptures:

And the LORD said to Satan, "Have you considered my servant Job, that there is none like him on the earth, a blameless and upright man, who fears God and turns away from evil?" Then Satan answered the LORD and said, "Does Job fear God for no reason? Have you not put a hedge around him and his house and all that he has, on every side? You have blessed the work of his hands, and his possessions have increased in the land. Job 1:8-10

WATCHMEN ON THE WALLS OF GOD'S HOUSE OF PRAYER

Through daily prayer, we strengthen the walls of our protection. As prayer warriors and watchmen on the walls of our households we also protect the lives of our loved ones and securing our ongoing victory through Christ.

We are called as followers of Christ to be watchmen on the walls of God's house as well as the households of the people of God. If we're not alert and watchful through prayer but asleep, we are like silent dogs who don't bark (Isaiah 56:10). God's house can't be without prayer warriors.

A prayerless church is a powerless church and without the life of Holy Spirit empowered prayers, that church will end up being dysfunctional. We should allow Jesus as our Lord and Saviour to awake the sleeping giant within us before it is too late. Are you ready to answer the call?

For thus the Lord said to me: "Go, set a watchman; let him announce what he sees.... Then he who saw cried out: "Upon a watchtower I stand, O Lord, continually by day, and at my post I am stationed whole nights. - Isaiah 21:6, 8

Awake, O sleeper, and arise from the dead, and Christ will shine on you. Ephesians 5:14b

Prayer is the breath of the church, the oxygen for the growth of the saints. We will pray more if we are more convicted about the power of prayer. This is how we fight our battles. Daily disciplined prayers will secure us against the schemes of our enemies.

Let's Pray!

APPLICATION

Write down three things you have learned from this Chapter:

____

____

____

____

____

Which truths have you learned that you will commit to apply in your devotion to God:

____

____

____

____

____

How and in what way will you apply this truth in your daily devotion?

____

____

____

____

____

Prayer:

Father God, thank You for equipping me with all it takes to defeat the enemy. Preserve me from all temptations and give me the wisdom to avoid all the schemes of the devil, in the mighty name of Jesus. Help me to always be on guard against the attacks and lies of the enemy. Amen.

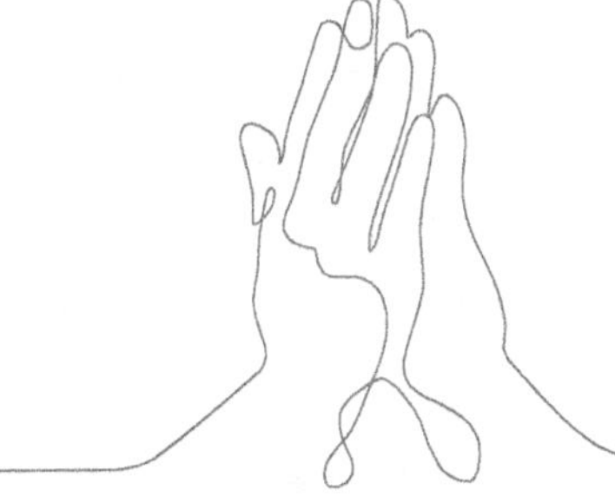

Chapter 12

For yours is the Kingdom,
the power, and the glory

YOURS IS THE KINGDOM, THE POWER, AND THE GLORY NOW AND FOREVER!

The end of the Lord's prayer serves as a reminder of the awesomeness of God, who is everlasting, eternal, all powerful and glorious. We may stop praying from time to time, but His kingdom, power and glory are unstoppable and ever-increasing. Therefore, our focus has to turn towards praising and worshiping the One we're in a covenant with.

So, our approach should be to remind God through praise and worship about who He said He will be for us. The Word of God often talks about reminding God of His promises, not because He is forgetful or unkind or withholding His goodness, but because He wants us to ask – in the same way a good parent wants their children to ask and make the desires of their hearts known to them. We've just prayed through many aspects of His character, will and kingdom, and now we are celebrating those truths. This should also remind us about who we are without Him, and how dependent we are upon His mercy and grace to get through every day.

If we understand and use this prayer correctly, we will be reminded about His kingdom, power and glory every day. The fact that we are in search after His kingdom and not ours, His power and glory above ours are vitally important.

Above all we have mentioned, we must realise that at the core of this kingdom, power and glory is a person, Jesus Christ, the one we're in love with. He is the King of all kings, the Lord of all lords, our Beloved. As we end this prayer, it should absolutely be our deepest desire to please Him. Thus, it will be helpful to allow His kingdom, power, and glory to reign in our hearts so that we are reminded about our true inheritance in Him.

HIS KINGDOM

- Praise Him because He has transferred us out of the kingdom of darkness and into the kingdom of His love and light.

- Submit to Him and ask Him to extend His rule and reign more and more in your life.

- Make this faith declaration about God's heavenly kingdom in your life.

"I will seek Your kingdom Lord with all my heart, mind and strength and I'm delighted that it's an everlasting kingdom. Your rule and reign will continue and crush all other ungodly kingdoms in my life. Today, I will advance Your kingdom and preach the Gospel to those who are lost. Lord, let Your kingdom increase in me."

HIS POWER

- Praise Him because He has saved you by His power through His love. He has invited you to be filled with the power of the Holy Spirit to be His witness.

- Submit the things that are currently difficult for you unto His power and allow Him to work miraculously on your behalf.

- Make this faith declaration about His power in your life.

"I am strong in the Lord and the power of His might, greater is He that lives in me than he that is in the world. I have been endued with power from on high to be His witness in the world. He gives power to the faint and keeps me by His power. He gives me power to be healthy and victorious, for He is my refuge and my fortress. I will dwell safely in the shelter of the Most High. Lord, let Your power increase in me."

HIS GLORY

- Praise Him for His glorious presence and peace in your life.

- Submit all earthly glories and your achievements to honour Him. Ask Him to allow His light to shine through you this day.

- Make this faith declaration about His glory in your life.

"The Lord will keep me and rescue me from every evil deed and bring me safely into his heavenly kingdom. Lord, reveal more of Your glory in my life and let Your peace that surpasses all understanding be with me. To him be the glory forever and ever. Amen!"

THE CALL OF THE BRIDE

The loving Father is inviting all His children as the Bride of His Son Jesus Christ to live a life worthy of His death and resurrection, a victorious church on earth, pure and holy unto Him. Let's pray that His invitation to us will not be wasted and in shame.

"Behold, I am coming soon, bringing my recompense with me, to repay each one for what he has done. I am the Alpha and the Omega, the first and the last, the beginning and the end." Blessed are those who wash their robes, so that they may have the right to the tree of life and that they may enter the city by the gates. The Spirit and the Bride say, "Come." And let the one who hears say, "Come." And let the one who is thirsty come; let the one who desires take the water of life without price." Revelation 22:12-14,17

Grace to you and peace from him who is and who was and who is to come, and from the seven spirits who are before his throne, and from Jesus Christ the faithful witness, the firstborn of the dead, and the ruler of kings on earth. To him who loves us and has freed us from our sins by his blood and made us a kingdom, priests to his God and Father, to him be glory and dominion forever and ever. Amen! Revelation 1:4-6

Now to him who is able to keep you from stumbling and to present you blameless before the presence of his glory with great joy, to the only God, our Saviour, through Jesus Christ our Lord, be glory, majesty, dominion, and authority, before all time and now and forever. Amen! Jude 1:24

We trust that from the discussion of prayer in this book, you will be encouraged to pray with a deeper intensity and that a culture of effective and sustainable prayer will be established in your heart.

We may stop praying from time to time, but His kingdom, power and glory which is unstoppable and ever-increasing will continue. Prayer is a powerful way to advance God's kingdom on earth. Therefore, our focus must turn towards praising and worshiping the One we're in a covenant with. The Lamb upon the throne, the worthy One who deserves all the glory.

Let's Pray!

APPLICATION

Write down three things you have learned from this Chapter:

____

____

____

____

____

Which truths have you learned that you will commit to apply in your devotion to God:

____

____

____

____

____

How and in what way will you apply this truth to your daily devotion?

____

____

____

____

____

Prayer:
Father God, I praise you for your faithfulness and power. You alone are worthy to receive all the glory, praise, and worship. Before you every knee will bow, and every tongue shall confess that you alone are Lord and King. Amen

Yours is the Kingdom, the power, and the glory now and forever!

PART THREE

HELP US TO PRAY

Chapter 13

Revival and prayer

WHAT IS REVIVAL?

Revival is a definite outcome if we are willing to obey and follow God's precedents. The aim of prayer is to bring about revival in the hearts of people and the gatherings of the church family.

> *If my people who are called by my name humble themselves, and pray and seek my face and turn from their wicked ways, then I will hear from heaven and will forgive their sin and heal their land. 2 Chronicles 7:14*

> *Will you not revive us again, that your people may rejoice in you?*
> *Psalm 85:6*

Let's use this quote from Duncan Campbell to define revival first:

"Revival is a community saturated with God."

God Encounters Ministries said:

"Revival is always preceded by prayer "

Arthur Wallis once said:

"At the heart of every revival is the spirit of prayer."

Revival is the spiritual awakening and restoration of the treasures of God's people and all men, by the power of the Holy Spirit, in their pursuit towards a deeper love for God. Revival is the metamorphosis of new life in every person that releases them from spiritual death to eternal life and a healthy, vibrant communion with God through Christ. It involves the renewal of our first love for God and the presence of God's Spirit.

"Revival as understood by most scholars is a corporate awakening of conscience and the consciousness of God. It leads to widespread repentance and renewal within the church and widespread repentance and salvation outside the church. It is generally thought to be a sovereign move of God within a society or a nation." Carol Gossman

"The awakening or quickening of God's people to their true nature and purpose." Robert Coleman.

"The return of the Church from her backslidings, and the conversion of sinners." Charles Finney

Revival and Prayer

The church in Acts experienced the power of revival. This was after days of continued prayer. "Humanly speaking, the church of Jesus Christ owes its very existence today to revivals." Throughout history, revivals have always been preceded by protracted seasons of prayer. After the resurrection, before Jesus ascended into heaven, He commanded His disciples to remain in Jerusalem and wait for the power of the Holy Spirit to come. This was not to be a period of just lazing around with little or nothing to do. They were to spend that time in prayer.

> *Behold, I send the Promise of My Father upon you; but tarry in the city of Jerusalem until you are endued with power from on high. Luke 24:49*

After Jesus' ascension, we are told that

> *... they returned to Jerusalem from the mount called Olivet, which is near Jerusalem, a Sabbath day's journey. These all continued with one accord in prayer and supplication, with the women and Mary the mother of Jesus, and with His brothers. Acts 1:12, 14*

One hundred and twenty of His disciples were in the upper room for ten days of extended prayer. Their prayer preceded the manifestation of the outpouring of the Holy Spirit as we know it. Revival is sustained by prayer and discipleship.

> *... they continued steadfastly in the apostles' doctrine and fellowship, in the breaking of bread, and in prayers. Acts 2:42 (ASV)*

It is interesting that the disciples spent days in prolonged prayer until the outpouring of the Holy Spirit that birthed the church. After the church was established, the disciples continued in the spirit of prayer and discipleship. The culture of prayer and discipleship was sustained throughout the book of Acts. The words *"prayer"*, *"prayers"*, *"prayed"*, *"praying"* and *"pray"* are found 29 times in the book of Acts.

The Protestant Reformation was preceded by prayer

The famous Protestant Reformation spearheaded by Martin Luther was born after he locked himself in a room, within the tower of the Black Monastery in Wittenberg for a season of sustained prayer and intense study of the Word. Without the power of prayer and the truth of God's Word, Luther would not have been able to go against the most powerful institution of his day, the Catholic church. The conviction of God's truth was strengthened by the time of fellowship he spent with God. That empowered him to resist the spiritual errors of the established church at the time.

John Wesley knew the power of prayer in quickening the move of God. He is credited with the popular saying:

"God does nothing but in answer to prayer; and even they who have been converted to God, without praying for it themselves (which is exceedingly rare), were not without the prayers of others. Every new victory which a soul gains is the effect of a new prayer."

John and Charles Wesley and George Whitfield spent hours in prayer, the Word and fasting. This resulted in the worldwide Methodist revival by the Wesley brothers. Also, the Great Awakening in America was born by George Whitefield. Another quote about revival says:

"God has given the pen of history into the hands of a praying church."
F. Kryskov

Revival of the Word and Spirit

A sound biblical foundation is what successful discipleship is built upon. Every revival that departs from the Word of God soon loses its relevance in the kingdom of God. To have a sustainable revival, the priority of the Word and the Spirit cannot be overemphasised. In the city of Ephesus, we see the revival of the Word and Spirit clearly. Paul spent two years in discipleship and teaching the converts to get them established in the Word.

> *And this continued for two years, so that all who dwelt in Asia heard the word of the Lord Jesus, both Jews and Greeks. Now God worked unusual miracles by the hands of Paul, so that even handkerchiefs or aprons were brought from his body to the sick, and the diseases left them and the evil spirits went out of them. Acts 19:10-12 (NKJV)*

A mighty revival of the Word and Spirit took place in Ephesus as seen in the above passage. To live in a continuous revival, we should embrace the Word and the Spirit of God in our lives. The Word provides us with a foundation and the Spirit brings the life and power of God.

Praying the Scriptures

If you abide in Me, and My words abide in you, you will ask what you desire, and it shall be done for you. John 15:7 (NKJV)

It is important to ensure that our prayers are always backed by the Word of God. God is committed to His Word, and He always stands His Word. When we base our prayers on God's Word, we will not ask for things that are contrary to his Word.

For people to continue to experience revival in their life, they must *"Abide"* in Christ. If we detach ourselves from Him, we will lose our fervour for Him. If we fail to remain in Him, we stand the risk of not having our prayers answered. Also, we need to allow His words to abide in us. He said, *"If you abide in Me and My Words abide in you..."*

When the Word of God finds a home in our hearts, praying the Scriptures becomes natural. That is when we begin to experience answers to our prayers. For instance, Jesus said, *"love your enemies..."* If that Word abides in us, we will not pray for God to kill your enemies.

Prayer brings the kingdom and the will of God into manifestation

Let us therefore come boldly unto the throne of grace that we may obtain mercy and find grace to help in a time of need. Hebrews 4:16 (NKJV)

Whenever there is debauchery and evil around us, it should motivate us to pray. Prayer changes things because it provokes God's intervention. Prayer allows us to come boldly into the throne room of the Father to ask and receive whatever we desire from Him in accordance with His will. Through prayer, we can move and obtain all the necessary help we need. We can, through prayer, *"speed up"* God's intervention in the earthly affairs of men. Read the story of how God intervened in Sodom and Gomorrah after Abraham's prayer (Genesis 18:22-33).

Revival is God's response to the prayers of the saints

Prayer is a spiritual means that enables us to access the Kingdom of Heaven. Prayer transcends boundaries and knows no limits. It is in the place of prayer that the will of God is enforced and that His Kingdom is made manifest on earth as it is in heaven. That is why, in Luke 11:2, Jesus instructs us to pray that *"Thy Kingdom come and let Thy Will be done."*

Jesus pointed out very specifically that we should pray for His kingdom to come. He didn't say preach or sing that Thy Kingdom come; he said PRAY that Thy Kingdom come. Somebody articulates it as follow:

"There have been revivals without much preaching, and there have been revivals with absolutely no organization, but there has never been a mighty revival without mighty prayer." [11]

Revival will not come without certain prerequisites

Revival is when the kingdom of God begins to manifest in our hearts, our families, our churches, our communities, our cities, and our nations. It is God's heart and will to revive mankind with His Word and Spirit and bring a spiritual awakening and change to the whole world. God is the author of revivals, and He has the final say in any revival. It will continue within His pre-planned timeline and within the regions He chooses. He is sovereign and from previous revivals we have seen that there are certain things that can quicken revivals. Whether it is personal, or within a church, or within a nation, it will be delayed unless we first apply some important principles in our hearts and churches.

In conclusion, let's look at five of these important truths and how the Bible explains it. These things are foundational predecessors for any revival to come.

1. Humility

> *.... if my people who are called by my name humble themselves, and pray and seek my face and turn from their wicked ways, then I will hear from heaven and will forgive their sin and heal their land. 2 Chronicles 7:14*

> *But he gives more grace. Therefore it says, "God opposes the proud but gives grace to the humble. James 4:7*

In the book, "The Leaven of Holiness, Conference for Religious," St Thomas said: *"In the order of virtues, humility holds the first rank in the sense that humility drives pride from us, (pride sets us at war with God) and that on the contrary, it renders man submissive and entirely open to the effusions of divine grace."*

---

11   Torrey, Reuben A. The Power of Prayer and the Prayer of Power

Revival begins with genuine humility. It takes humility to acknowledge our bankruptcy without God and thus to seek God. It's very interesting that God doesn't oppose the sinner, but it is the pride that He opposes.

2. The Lordship of Jesus Christ

Lordship is a heart matter. The Lordship of Christ has to do with His supreme authority in our life. To experience revival, it is important to not only acknowledge the supremacy of Christ, but to completely obey Him in all things.

> Let all the house of Israel therefore know for certain that God has made him both Lord and Christ, this Jesus whom you crucified." Now when they heard this they were cut to the heart, and said to Peter and the rest of the apostles, "Brothers, what shall we do?" Acts 2:36-37

> Therefore, as you received Christ Jesus the Lord, so walk in him, rooted and built up in him and established in the faith, just as you were taught, abounding in thanksgiving. Colossians 2:6-7

3. Turn away from sin as a fruit of repentance

> Repent therefore, and turn back, that your sins may be blotted out, that times of refreshing may come from the presence of the Lord, and that he may send the Christ appointed for you, Jesus, whom heaven must receive until the time for restoring all the things about which God spoke by the mouth of his holy prophets long ago. Acts 3:19-21

> Thus it is written, that Christ should suffer and on the third day rise from the dead, and that repentance for the forgiveness of sins should be proclaimed in his name to all nations, beginning from Jerusalem. You are witnesses of these things. Luke 24:46-48

Repentance is the entry point into the kingdom of God. Without it, you cannot experience God's best. When people see the true state of their sinful hearts, and turn to God in repentance, revival begins in their hearts.

4. Yielding to the purifying power of the Holy Spirit

> I baptize you with water for repentance, but he who is coming after me is mightier than I, whose sandals I am not worthy to carry. He will baptize you with the Holy Spirit and fire. His winnowing fork is in his hand, and he will clear his threshing floor and gather his wheat into the barn, but the chaff he will burn with unquenchable fire. Matthew 3:11-12

And suddenly there came from heaven a sound like a mighty rushing wind, and it filled the entire house where they were sitting. And divided tongues as of fire appeared to them and rested on each one of them. And they were all filled with the Holy Spirit and began to speak in other tongues as the Spirit gave them utterance. Acts 2:2-4

The Holy Spirit brings a fire that either purifies or consumes. In revival, the Holy Spirit purifies our hearts of things that defile us and sets us on fire and makes us effective witnesses for Jesus. This is a work that requires our cooperation.

5. Total surrender and consecration of our hearts

Get up! Consecrate the people and say, 'Consecrate yourselves for tomorrow; for thus says the LORD, God of Israel, "There are devoted things in your midst, O Israel. You cannot stand before your enemies until you take away the devoted things from among you." Joshua 7:13

And for their sake I consecrate myself, that they also may be sanctified in truth. John 17:19

Surrender being a military word, denotes the relinquishing of your rights and weapons to the conqueror. Jesus has fought and won the right to the total surrender of our hearts and plans in exchange for His. Through consecration, we set ourselves apart for the service of our Lord and Saviour. To experience continuous revival, a lifestyle of total surrender and consecration cannot be overemphasised.

"Prayer will promote our personal holiness as nothing else except the study of the Word of God." [12]

Let's pray!

---

12 Torrey, Reuben A. The Power of Prayer and the Prayer of Power

APPLICATION

Write down three things you have learned from this Chapter:

____

____

____

____

Which truths have you learned that you will commit to apply in your devotion to God:

____

____

____

____

How and in what way will you apply this truth to your daily devotion?

____

____

____

____

Prayer:
Thank you, Lord, for the move of Your Spirit in my heart. Let this fire in my heart translate to the fulfilment of the Great Commission and the transformation of communities, in the mighty name of Jesus. Lord, I ask that you bring a revival in me, by the Spirit and Word of God. Amen.

Chapter **14**

Effective Prayer

It is possible to pray effectively. Yes, it is possible to receive Godly wisdom about our daily interests, and to walk in His counsel every day. Effective prayer does not have to be difficult and beyond our reach. In fact, one of the main reasons why God gave us the Holy Spirit is to help us to pray. Prayer is enabled by the Holy Spirit who dwells in the children of God. God is Spirit, and we must connect with His wisdom through our born-again spirits, through which the Holy Spirit dwells.

> *Likewise the Spirit helps us in our weakness. For we do not know what to pray for as we ought, but the Spirit himself intercedes for us with groanings too deep for words. And he who searches hearts knows what is the mind of the Spirit, because the Spirit intercedes for the saints according to the will of God. Romans 8:26-27*

The Holy Spirit wants to teach us how He would pray through us according to the will of God. He is present and available to every believer, and He wants to reveal Jesus to them, lead them into all truth, and give them a powerful, and effective prayer life.

The Spirit of Prayer

Whenever we approach God in prayer and He touches our hearts, it should be normal to feel overwhelmed in such a way that we find ourselves at a place where we don't know what or how to pray. God loves it when we are dependent and broken before Him. As Andrew Murray said:

"That's when the Holy Spirit works, and His secret working place, the place where all work must begin, is in the heart where He comes to teach a man how to pray." [13]

When pursuing and facilitating prayer we must understand that effective prayers are whirling and ignited by a *'spirit of prayer.'* The spirit of prayer is the opposite of all other spirits in the heavenly realms and this world. Our battles are not against flesh and blood and therefore we should be strong in the Lord and in the strength of His might (Ephesians 6:10). The *'spirit of prayer'* partners well with the *'spirit of faith and courage'* when we pray.

---

13 Murray, Andrew. The Master's Indwelling

Since we have the same spirit of faith according to what has been written, "I believed, and so I spoke," we also believe, and so we also speak, knowing that he who raised the Lord Jesus will raise us also with Jesus and bring us with you into his presence. 2 Corinthians 4:13-14

God's breath [ruach] should be the fuel within our hearts exploding through us to pray mighty prayers. The Holy Spirit is the motivator and passion needed in all our prayers to lift our spirits above the spirit of fear, anxiety, disappointment etc.

And I will pour on the house of David and on the inhabitants of Jerusalem the Spirit of grace and supplication; then they will look on Me whom they pierced. Yes, they will mourn for Him as one mourns for his only son, and grieve for Him as one grieves for a firstborn. Zechariah 12:10 NKJV

Not by might, nor by power, but by my Spirit, says the LORD of hosts. Zechariah 4:6b

The Holy Spirit will not only help us in *'how to pray'* but also ignites us to pray. God will pour out *'the Spirit of grace and supplication; then they will look on Me whom they pierced.'* (John 19:37) Such a beautiful piece of scripture! It is only by His grace that we are enabled to look at Him in times of mourning and make supplications to Him. It's by His Spirit that we prevail and conquer our adversaries; it's by His Spirit that we intercede for others, it's by His Spirit that we pray effectively.

Effective prayers start with the divine knowledge and revelation of the unity that we find within the Trinity.

"What we know and believe about God will affect how we pray. And if we're on shaky ground about who God is we will struggle with unbelief, lack of faith and doubt. We will be tossed around like children by their circumstances, trials, politics, economics etc. or we may end up not praying at all." (Julie-Anne Bartleet notes)

Sometimes we may feel that there is no difference if we pray or not, or we may say: *"Is it really possible to talk to God and get answers?"*

A lifestyle of effectual prayer is born from a growing intimacy with Jesus Christ. We must desire a daily personal relationship with Jesus that is at the same time intimate and powerful so that we can please God in our prayers and live in His power and wisdom.

The Gospel is the ultimate answer to all our prayers

If the Spirit of God is our teacher in how to pray effectively, we should know that we receive the fullness of the Spirit after a born again encounter with Jesus and the baptism in the Holy Spirit.

Without the Gospel, it is impossible to connect with God, and so receive His wisdom. Through the Gospel, God intervenes in earthly matters and makes it possible for mankind to communicate and walk with God like Adam did. Remember, Jesus is the only way to the Father. Any stability in life between mankind and God depends on the grace of God.

"At the core of the Gospel is a God of love, who came down to mankind in the form of His Son, He lived the life we should have lived and died the death we should have died, in our place. He rose from the dead proving that He is the Son of God and offering the gift of salvation and forgiveness of sins to anyone who repents and believes in Him." (Dr. Rice Broocks)

If He was willing to intervene in our salvation, why will He not intervene to help in our daily circumstances (Rom 8:32). All authority belongs to Him, and through prayer we are empowered to take part in the greatest work God has for us and the world.

Prayer is the cutting edge of any of God's work; it releases God to do what He longs to do - we partner with Him in His plans for this generation and the generations to come, and He prepares us to rule and reign with Him for all eternity. When He commanded us to go and make disciples of all nations and to teach them what He taught us, He promised to be with us until the end. His name is Immanuel, God with us!

Help us to pray

To know there is help available and to pray effectively is such great news and it releases us from a lot of pressure and self-effort. It is natural for us to think that we should pray from our thoughts and be guided by our own wisdom and feelings, because we are human. However, we should never forget that God gave us His Spirit to help us to pray. That is why it is imperative that we surrender ourselves to be His instruments of prayer.

The Bible teaches that the prayers of the saints are as incense unto God (Rev 5:8, 8:3), and leaves a delightful fragrance of our surrendered hearts before His throne.

We as Christians were saved because of the prayers of others. Why not pray for more people to be saved?

Mary broke the alabaster flask of expensive ointment made from pure nard and anointed the head and feet of Jesus and wiped his feet with her hair. The house was filled with the fragrance of the perfume (John 12:3). Our prayers are like the oil that runs down on His body, a delightful fragrance of the saints. Jesus rebuked the disciples when they wanted to stop her and said: *"wherever the gospel is proclaimed in the whole world, what she has done will be told in memory of her."* (Matthew 26:13) I still remember the day God's Spirit said to me:

"A prayer without surrender is a prayer without a pulse!"

Throughout the Bible we see how people responded to God as He reveals Himself through His creation as well as direct communication through the prophets, kings and priests, and their response to Him in their varying degrees of obedience. Prayer is a two-way communication with a single purpose - to honor the One who is worthy.

God answers all prayers

Most believers understand that the Word of God teaches that the purpose of prayer is to receive answers and wisdom from God. This is true and part of our motivation, because God promised that He will answer us when we call to Him (Psalm 91:15).

> *If I had cherished iniquity in my heart, the Lord would not have listened. But truly God has listened; he has attended to the voice of my prayer. Blessed be God, because he has not rejected my prayer or removed his steadfast love from me! Psalm 66:18-20*

Now, if God promised to answer, then we should be willing to accept His answer and believe that He always answers our prayers. The difficult part is to understand and commit to God's answers, because God has many ways of answering our prayers. Let me say it again. God hears and answers prayer - we should believe it and not measure God, based on the outcomes of our prayers. We must make peace with the fact that we can't rush God, nor manipulate Him or end up justifying our frustration. God is God, unchanging, ever true, and always the same. The problem with unanswered prayers is not with God. We must believe that God answers prayer as the ultimate conviction of truth (Matthew 6:8).

God's answers to our prayers are God's wisdom in our lives. His wisdom will always benefit us. A very well-known scripture in the Bible, which is used by many believers, to find peace regarding life issues and answers to prayer is Romans 8:28:

And we know that for those who love God all things work together for good, for those who are called according to his purpose.

When reading it within its context we would realize that it has to do with the Holy Spirit teaching us to pray and finding God's will as the answer to our prayers. Because God loves us unconditionally and if we serve Him unconditionally in total surrender, His wisdom and answers will always turn out for the good, to benefit us most.

God's wisdom and answers come to us in the same way as the use of traffic lights in our communities. To smoothly control traffic, we use traffic lights. These lights have three colours - red, yellow, and green, that communicate stop, wait, and go. It works perfectly while honoured, but we still have accidents when people disregard these signs. In the same way we will have smooth transitions in life when following Godly wisdom. But if not, we will experience accidents and trouble that is often discouraging and stops us from praying.

God is attentive to our prayers. He hears our prayers and sees our hearts. His answers are not always a green light, but He always works things out for our good because He loves us, and He is faithful to His plans for our lives. Let's look at what the Bible teaches.

But the wisdom from above is first pure, then peaceable, gentle, open to reason, full of mercy and good fruits, impartial and sincere. James 3:17

All the prayers that Jesus prayed were answered and Jesus is our example. If we pray correctly and according to His will, we will experience His perfect answer to our prayers. If we ask according to His will, He hears. If He hears then He answers according to our petition.

Praying according to God's will is the only way in scripture that we will receive from Him.

And this is the confidence that we have toward him, that if we ask anything according to his will he hears us. And if we know that he hears us in whatever we ask, we know that we have the requests that we have asked of him. 1 John 5:14-15

Having confidence in prayer is a key to receiving answers. Asking and receiving according to God's will as well as understanding God's will resonates with each other.

People have asked: *"What is God's will?"* or *"How do I know it is God's will for me to have what I am asking Him?"* or *"Maybe the reason I did not receive what I asked from God was because it was not His will for me."* Some people may think God has favourites. To bring some light to these difficult questions, we should read 1 John 3:21-22

> *Beloved, if our heart does not condemn us, we have confidence before God; and whatever we ask we receive from him, because we keep his commandments and do what pleases him.*

Keeping His commandments will have a direct influence on our prayers being answered. Obedience to God's Word and faith in Him will position us to receive answers from God. To obey God is, in a sense, His love language. The issue of unanswered prayers relates directly to the wrong love issues in our lives.

"He demands that we listen to His Word before He listens to our prayers."[14]

The prophet Isaiah points out a very important matter concerning God answering our prayers.

> *Behold, the LORD'S hand is not shortened, that it cannot save, or his ear dull, that it cannot hear; but your iniquities have made a separation between you and your God, and your sins have hidden his face from you so that he does not hear. Isaiah 59:1-2*

Our involvement in sin will have a negative influence on our prayer life. Sin will make God's ear dull and shorten His hand to save us, but through Jesus as our Mediator, we can conquer sin and pray to the Father without any limitations. We should always remember that God is holy and we're not, He will never allow the power of sin to rule over our right standing in Christ Jesus. God is sovereign and His grace abounds, but we should not allow sin to prevent us from enjoying answered prayers. He already sent a ransom for sin, but we must follow His ways.

---

14 Torrey, Reuben A. The Power of Prayer and the Prayer of Power

That's why we must connect with the Father through Jesus and His redemptive offering for our sins. Interesting that God's ear and His hand are connected in this scripture for our salvation to come.

A lifestyle of sin will prevent God from answering us and will bring separation between us. But if we come to Him in true humility and repentance, He will forgive us our sins and answer our prayers. (1 John 1:5-10)

"The basic purpose of prayer is NOT to bend God's will to mine, but to mould my will into His." Tim Keller

Let's never forget to celebrate the privilege of approaching a holy God through Jesus Christ in prayer. Let's enjoy His presence and allow Him more and more to intervene in our lives every day. Let's trust God for daily sincere encounters as we pray to establish eternal values in our hearts to live God fearing lives. May we grow from participants in prayer to warriors who experience God's wisdom through prayer. Always remember that the condition of our hearts counts before God.

Effective prayer is not about the words we use nor the time we spend but the heart we apply. PW Coffee

May we enjoy asking God according to His will and God answering our prayers. May God not only answer our prayers but also our questions concerning prayer. May we live our lives in obedience towards His commandments; aiming to please Him in everything we do.

"A man with an experience of God is never at the mercy of an argument."
PD Le Roux

Remember God is not a faraway God or someone to distance us from Him. When we draw near to Him, He will draw near to us to manifest His presence in our midst. God desires for us to experience Him every day.

Let's pray!

APPLICATION

Write down three things you have learned from this Chapter:

____

____

____

____

Which truths have you learned that you will commit to apply in your devotion to God:

____

____

____

____

How and in what way will you apply this truth to your daily devotion?

____

____

____

____

Prayer:
Father God, thank you for the spirit of prayer in my life. Show me how to be consistently and effective in prayer. Amen.

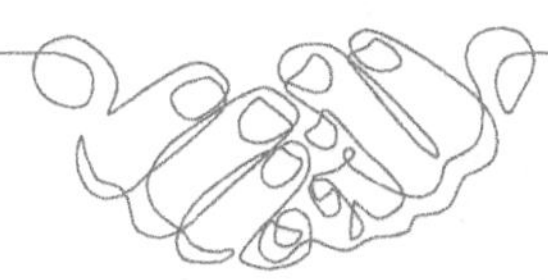

Chapter 15

Building blocks
to answered prayers

BUILDING BLOCKS TO ANSWERED PRAYERS

Building blocks are something we use to build a strong structure on a firm foundation. Prayers that are Spirit empowered and based on the Word of God, will have a strong foundation, and will turn out to be effective prayers. We must adapt our hearts and minds to praying for a solution based on God's Word rather than praying for the desires of our hearts. The Spirit can enlighten our minds and give new birth to our inheritance in Christ and bring forth the kingdom of God through the power of the Word while we pray.

> *And when they had prayed, the place in which they were gathered together was shaken, and they were all filled with the Holy Spirit and continued to speak the word of God with boldness. Acts 4:31*

The Spirit and the Word work together to ensure effective results. With the Word of God as our foundation (Hebrew 4:12), we must also apply certain principles as building blocks for an effective prayer. Below is a list of these building blocks that will better define the ingredients of effective prayer. We will find that effective prayer always reverts to one thing - our devotion to God. Praying through these accompanying scriptures will establish a stronger devotion to God.

1. Devoted to God

Jesus' devotion to the Father in everything He did was the key to effective ministry. Even when He had to face Satan, while He was tempted in the desert; He entered in the power of the Spirit (after water baptism) and spoke the Word of God to seal His victory. (Matthew 4:1-11) The first disciples devoted themselves to God in more than one way (Acts 2:42).

They devoted themselves:

- To the apostles' teachings
- To fellowship with other believers
- To the breaking of bread
- To prayer initiatives

2. A pure, humble, and repentant heart

Our prayers are influenced by the condition of our hearts. Pure hearts produce pure motives and those who are pure in heart will see God (Matthew 5:8).

> *Repent, therefore, of this wickedness of yours, and pray to the Lord that, if possible, the intent of your heart may be forgiven you. Acts 8:22*

Our hearts serve as a place where the kingdom of God enters and is established into our lives. His kingdom and will has to first work in us, before it works through us. Out of the fullness of the heart the mouth speaks (Luke 6:45)

> *Who shall ascend the hill of the LORD? And who shall stand in his holy place? He who has clean hands and a pure heart. Psalm 24:3-4*

> *let us draw near with a true heart in full assurance of faith, with our hearts sprinkled clean from an evil conscience and our bodies washed with pure water. Hebrews 10:22*

> *Draw near to God, and he will draw near to you. Cleanse your hands, you sinners, and purify your hearts, you double-minded...... Humble yourselves before the Lord, and he will exalt you. James 4:8,10*

Humility comes before unity and if we desire God's intervention, we should earnestly humble our hearts before Him. Let God be God, always.

3. A surrendered will

For God's will to come, our will has to be surrendered unto Him. Our way of seeing and interpreting things can become either a building block or a stumbling block to our prayers. Our devotion to Him will determine in whom we will put our trust and who we will follow. We have to surrender our desires and plans to Him.

> *But he gives more grace. Therefore it says, "God opposes the proud but gives grace to the humble." Submit yourselves therefore to God. Resist the devil, and he will flee from you. James 4:6-7*

4. Appetite for the things of God

Seeking after God and His kingdom in everything we think, speak, and do will establish a deeper devotion towards Him. To desire God and His presence more than anything else in our lives is at the core of a consecrated lifestyle. Whenever anyone wants to buy or make use of a good or service, there is usually a price attached, and every kingdom has a currency. Spiritual hunger and thirst are both currencies of the kingdom of God. These will expand our capacity for more of God. Regular fasting to strengthen our focus on the things above will replace worldly appetites and the desires of the flesh with Godly desires.

> *The hand of our God is for good on all who seek him, and the power of his wrath is against all who forsake him." So we fasted and implored our God for this, and he listened to our entreaty. Ezra 8:22b*

> *Then I turned my face to the Lord God, seeking him by prayer and pleas for mercy with fasting and sackcloth and ashes. I prayed to the LORD my God and made confession, saying, "O Lord, the great and awesome God, who keeps covenant and steadfast love with those who love him and keep his commandments. Daniel 9:3-4*

Even in the gathering of the saints, the early church served God with passion and eagerness to obey, and regular gatherings for discipleship and prayers was the norm. (Hebrews 10:23-15, Act 2:42-47)

5. True worship

Devotion to God is like inhaling oxygen, while worship is exhaling our awe and praise to Him. Worship is seen as surrendering to God, but with it goes the sacrificing and laying down of our lives for His purposes. Many of the Old Testament heroes of faith, built altars where they worshiped God, especially after victories on the battlefields. It was during these times of surrender and prayer that God revealed more of Himself and established His covenant truths deeper within their hearts. Our worship displays our reverence and honour for who we love.

> *Then the LORD appeared to Abram and said, "To your offspring I will give this land." So he built there an altar to the LORD, who had appeared to him. From there he moved to the hill country .... And there he built an altar to the LORD and called upon the name of the LORD. Genesis 12:7-8*

And Moses built an altar and called the name of it, The LORD Is My Banner! Exodus 17:15

In the days of his flesh, Jesus offered up prayers and supplications, with loud cries and tears, to him who was able to save him from death, and he was heard because of his reverence. Hebrews 5:7

God is spirit, and those who worship him must worship in spirit and truth. John 4:24

6. A commitment to regular prayer

Prayer is a spiritual discipline and without proper commitment to pray we will struggle to keep up with a life of effective prayer. Jesus said, *"could you not watch one hour?"* (Mark 14:37). The first disciples gathered at the *"hour of prayer"* (Acts 3:1) We should discipline ourselves to pray. It does not come only through a desire to pray but through discipline.

Rejoice in hope, be patient in tribulation, be constant in prayer. Romans 12:12

...pray without ceasing, 1 Thessalonians 5:17

7. A commitment towards reading the Word of God

As little children we sang the song; "Read your Bible, pray every day, pray every day .... and it is so necessary to have it as a custom in our daily devotion. David declared that the Word of God is a lamp unto his feet and a light unto his path (Psalm 119:105). By following the precepts of His Word, we will sin less. Living according to the Word of God will cause our lives to align with His thoughts and plans for us. His Word is His truth.

"If anyone loves me, he will keep my word, and my Father will love him, and we will come to him and make our home with him. John 14:23

But we will devote ourselves to prayer and to the ministry of the word." Acts 6:4

Sanctify them in the truth; your word is truth. John 17:17

8. Faith

Mountain moving faith, fighting the good fight of faith, the righteous who live by faith, righteousness through faith and many more, are all terms used in the New Testament. The Bible defines faith as the assurance of things hoped for, the conviction of things not seen (Hebrews 11:1). A faithless prayer will keep us in the realm of reality, but a faith filled prayer will unleash the faithfulness of God towards us.

> *Therefore I tell you, whatever you ask in prayer, believe that you have received it, and it will be yours. Mark 11:24*

> *And the prayer of faith will save the one who is sick, and the Lord will raise him up. And if he has committed sins, he will be forgiven. James 5:15*

9. Hope

Having hope in a hopeless world or situations is necessary for us to pray effectively. Faith is numb without hope and cannot operate effectively for righteous outcomes for faith and hope must work together in tandem. Hope anchors the soul; it serves as the draft picture of what needs to manifest. Hope is the substance of our faith, the assurance of things we pray, and the conviction of things not seen yet. (Hebrews 11:1) Hope empowers our prayers and encourages us to be constant in prayer.

> *Rejoice in hope, be patient in tribulation, be constant in prayer. Romans 12:12*

10. Persistence

> *And he told them a parable to the effect that they ought always to pray and not lose heart. Luke 18:1*

The apostle Luke mentioned two stories Jesus told about being persistent that is not found in the other three gospel accounts. (Luke 11:5-8 and 18:1-8) In both comparisons we find someone in need and asking for help. The one refers to a friend while the other refers to an unrighteous judge. In both these cases the attention to their asking was delayed but they demanded an answer with persistence.

> *I tell you, though he will not get up and give him anything because he is his friend, yet because of his impudence he will rise and give him whatever he needs. Luke 11:8*

yet because this widow keeps bothering me, I will give her justice, so that she will not beat me down by her continual coming.'" And the Lord said, "Hear what the unrighteous judge says. Luke 18:5-6

The word *"impudence"* in Luke 11:8 can also be translated as persistence or shamelessness. Persistence goes beyond friendship or injustice because it is connected to unquenchable faith in God found in our righteousness before Him. We can approach God without shame because of Jesus. Therefore, we can place a demand on the keys of the kingdom to unlock the doors of heaven and bring us breakthroughs.

11. A commitment to follow in obedience

'Following God in obedience' and 'abiding in the Vine' are two very similar terms. To abide means, to walk in proximity with God. We abide in Him through obedience and follow in His footsteps wholeheartedly. Obedience is a matter of the heart, a condition that is determined by who or what is sitting on the throne of our lives. It reflects through our thoughts, our deeds, and words. It is important to remember that our prayers are affected by our obedience.

We have to serve our Master with an ongoing "YES" every day. The only words that fit well before the word Lord, are yes or no. Let's soften our hearts and cultivate within our lives an ongoing 'Yes Lord' through our prayers. Jesus asked two blind men if they believe that He can heal them, they answered Him, "Yes Lord" (Matthew 9:27-29).

Beloved, if our heart does not condemn us, we have confidence before God; and whatever we ask we receive from him, because we keep his commandments and do what pleases him. 1 John 3:21-22

If you abide in Me, and My words abide in you, you will ask what you desire, and it shall be done for you. John 15:7

The end of all things is at hand; therefore be self-controlled and sober-minded for the sake of your prayers. 1 Peter 4:7

12. A commitment towards reconciliation

The love of God and everything relating to the Gospel is explained in Jesus' willingness as the Son of God, to leave heaven and come to earth to reconcile mankind with the Father. He prayed while hanging on the cross;

"Father forgive them...." The spirit of reconciliation will stir the fear of God in our lives. A reconciled heart is an attribute of the new creation in Christ.

All this is from God, who through Christ reconciled us to himself and gave us the ministry of reconciliation; that is, in Christ God was reconciling the world to himself, not counting their trespasses against them, and entrusting to us the message of reconciliation. 2 Corinthians 5:18-19

So if you are offering your gift at the altar and there remember that your brother has something against you, leave your gift there before the altar and go. First be reconciled to your brother, and then come and offer your gift. Matthew 5:32-24

And whenever you stand praying, forgive, if you have anything against anyone, so that your Father also who is in heaven may forgive you your trespasses." Mark 11:25

13. Boldness to pray

In Acts 3:1-10 we find a beautiful story of how Peter and John act in boldness through praying for a begging crippled man on their way to the temple. They said: *"Look at us...I have no silver and gold, but what I do have I give to you. In the name of Jesus Christ of Nazareth, rise up and walk!"*

We too have so many opportunities every day, to pray for people. We should be eager to connect life's difficult circumstances with the glory of God through prayer. Looking for more opportunities to pray will ignite a deeper desire towards prayer.

And when they had prayed, the place in which they were gathered together was shaken, and they were all filled with the Holy Spirit and continued to speak the word of God with boldness. Acts 4:31

I desire then that in every place the men should pray, lifting holy hands without anger or quarreling; 1 Timothy 2:8

14. Healthy Biblical marriages

It is very interesting how the unity within the marriage relationship can promote answered prayers of the husbands. Should it be because God compares the marriage relationship with unconditional love between the Bridegroom and the bride? Paul said this is a mystery to honour each other and live with mutual respect.

Likewise, husbands, live with your wives in an understanding way, showing honor to the woman as the weaker vessel, since they are heirs with you of the grace of life, so that your prayers may not be hindered. 1 Peter 3:7

15. Praying in the Holy Spirit

In closing, let us touch on the topic of praying in tongues. The Bible teaches that there is a clear difference between speaking in tongues and praying in tongues. Paul himself admitted that he prayed in tongues more than anyone else in the Corinthian church. He promotes it as a spiritual encouragement to the human spirit and says that when we do so, we pray the mysteries of God. (1 Corinthians 14:2)

After many experiences of breakthroughs through praying the mysteries of God, and praying in tongues, it will change your opinion about this custom. This is a powerful habit that simultaneously will build up believers and chase away demons. We should pray things through.

"The two great secrets of prevailing prayer are praying in the name of the Lord Jesus and praying in the Holy Spirit." [15]

When I pray in the Spirit, I try to visualize the situation I'm praying into. Then I zoom in on my intention and sometimes my emotions on this matter. Then with much boldness and faith in the almighty God, I start praying in the Spirit knowing that I do pray the mysteries and oracles of God into this matter.

But you, beloved, building yourselves up in your most holy faith and praying in the Holy Spirit, keep yourselves in the love of God, waiting for the mercy of our Lord Jesus Christ that leads to eternal life. Jude 1:20-21

... praying at all times in the Spirit, with all prayer and supplication. To that end, keep alert with all perseverance, making supplication for all the saints, Ephesians 6:18

"Praying in the Spirit is going into the unseen future to sort out things before they arrive." Eric Bapetel

Let's pray!

---

15 Torrey, Reuben A. The Power of Prayer and the Prayer of Power

APPLICATION

Write down three things you have learned from this Chapter:

____

____

____

____

Which truths have you learned that you will commit to apply in your devotion to God:

____

____

____

____

How and in what way will you apply this truth to your daily devotion?

____

____

____

____

Prayer:
Heavenly Father, I want to be fully committed to a lifestyle of prayer. Help me to make prayer a culture in my life and home, in the name of Jesus. Amen.

Chapter 16

Stumbling blocks
to answered prayers

STUMBLING BLOCKS TO ANSWERED PRAYERS

Stumbling blocks are *'circumstances that cause difficulty or hesitation'*[16] and there are many.

In this chapter we will list some of them so that we are able to identify them and as a result conquer them. We should not allow these things to steal our focus or limit our faith while praying. We must pray from a place of victory through Jesus and overcome these stumbling blocks.

Looking at the sermon on the mount and the topics Jesus touched on; after providing His disciples and us with a prayer model, we can easily put together a list of stumbling blocks that can hinder a praying culture within us. What we should notice is that Jesus continued straight after He taught them how to pray and immediately started to point out these issues. These hindrances are growing like fruits on the trees of human lives, and it will be wrong to merely try and cut off the fruits without dealing with the roots of these trees. (Matthew 6:19-7:12)

Jesus ends the teaching on prayer with Matthew 7:11 where He reiterates the commitment of the good Father who gives His children the things they ask for. He also points out that how we treat others will have an impact on our prayers. The conclusion of the Law and the Prophets is about our love for God and our love for one another. Without discipleship, people easily become false prophets, pretending to lead the morally right life but bearing different fruit.

Below is a list of stumbling blocks that will prevent prayers from being answered. This is not to condemn anyone but to help us understand how much we need God's grace in life. These hindrances are not always clear to find and can easily overlap and many times are difficult to overcome.

The good news is that we do have a Helper, the Holy Spirit who will help us to pray because Jesus has already paid the full price for us to be victorious in life and enjoy fruitful answered prayers.

---

16   Google definition

PRIDE

Pride is the root of all sin and is so powerful that it didn't just steal Satan's worship and devotion to God; it cost him his place in heaven. God is absolutely against all forms of pride.

When we allow pride to rule in our hearts, we give Satan and the forces of darkness an opening to launch attacks on us. Pride will cause our dependence on God to decrease and our trust to move towards self-effort. Therefore, pride results in us not wanting to pray to God and await His help.

A Dutch proverb says:

"Sinning will make a man leave off praying, or praying will make a man leave off sinning."

The only way to overcome pride is to submit to God, to recognize that we need His abounding grace which He will give to those who are humble. He is a jealous God who deserves our complete reverence.

> *But he gives more grace. Therefore it says, "God opposes the proud but gives grace to the humble. James 4:6*

CATEGORY 1: RELATIONAL ISSUES

Scriptures: Matthew 6:14-15; 7:1-5

Displayed as: All the different kinds of unforgiveness issues between mankind and God as well as person to person. Unforgiveness is one of the main stumbling blocks in unanswered prayer. Forgiving and being forgiven are inseparable. The ability to forgive others is made easier by the understanding that we are too forgiven and accepted by God in Jesus Christ. People who can't overcome guilt, rejection, and offence from God and people will experience defeat. Prayer will help us learn to love others unconditionally. People who struggle to find their new identity in Christ and who live from their new freedom as a child of God are very hard on themselves and live with a slave mentality. They struggle to build new relationships and to trust people and God. They believe they deserve to suffer or fall short of God's glory.

Prayer is communication with God and our relational issues create a distance between us and God. God is a relational Father and when people struggle to fix or maintain healthy relationships they struggle with prayer. In this way the intimacy is broken, and the relationship tends to become more like a religious duty than enjoyment.

Unresolved issues can easily turn into anger and resentment where people start to demand instead of being content. Judgemental opinions and negative attitudes dominate the speech and general viewpoints of these people.

Human responses: Unforgiveness, anger, manipulation, isolation, racism, judging people, disappointment in people, low self-esteem, bitterness.

CATEGORY 2: EARTHLY TREASURES

Scripture: Matthew 6:19-21

Displayed as: A worldly temporary focusing, trusting, or holding onto earthly treasures. People who are worried and anxious about the value of their earthly treasures and what they have in life will find it difficult to share or be generous towards others or God. They will struggle with what they lose rather than what they will gain when it comes to the kingdom of God.

Overall, they will find it difficult to submit to the Lordship of Jesus and will have trust issues. These people will struggle with the Sovereignty of God or lack faith to pray. Their mindset is focused on earthly treasures. They are very self-righteous and many times there are unconfessed sins that are hidden, and they don't want to deal with it, therefore their prayers will be hindered (Psalm 66:18). In many ways they find it challenging to honour other people and their successes. Competition dominates their actions.

Human responses: Selfishness, self-righteousness, sinful lifestyle, unconfessed sins, prideful decisions, bragging attitude, greedy practices, discontent with what they have, complaining unnecessarily, negative speech, disregard for others.

CATEGORY 3: WRONG PERSPECTIVES

Scripture: Matthew 6:22-23

Displayed as: An unbiblical perspective or viewpoint of God, yourselves, different people, Satan, and devilish practices as well as an unbiblical worldview. These are negative people who display a confused perspective of life issues, who struggle to be flexible, and always delay decision making.

- **A wrong perspective of the Godhead/Trinity - (Father, Son, and the Holy Spirit)**

God is - uncreated, eternal, a Triune supreme Spirit being, Creator of all that exists. He is the Almighty, all-powerful, all-knowing, the great I Am, holy, sovereign, Deliverer, Redeemer of man; just to mention a few. He can be known as Creator to mankind, but only Father to believers and followers of Jesus Christ, for it is by the Holy Spirit that we cry "Abba, Father!" (Graeme Goldsworthy)

These are three persons in such unity that they are called One. The reality of prayer is found in the communication of the Trinity before there were ever people to pray to God. The Father, Son and Holy Spirit have communicated from all eternity and are now reflected in our being created in His image as speaking, communicating beings. Our sin has cut us off from that conversational circle.

The source of prayer is the Fatherhood of God, who works all things according to His sovereign will and allows us to share in that by working through our prayers. The basis of our prayer is the Sonship of Jesus, we share in it when we are united to Him through faith. Jesus can address the Father and is heard, so we in Jesus Christ can address the Father and be heard. Praying in the "Family name" that's what it means to pray in the Name of Jesus.

- **A wrong perspective of yourself and others**

Mankind was created in the image and likeness of God, for His purpose, not vice versa. We must prioritize everything about us with an eternal perspective.

- **A wrong perspective of Satan**

"God and Satan are not opposites – that's the heathen/pagan view. They are not equal counterparts. Satan is a created spirit being who rebelled against God and was thrown out of Heaven. He is our adversary, not God's. Jesus has defeated Him, and we walk in that victory, although the battle continues to be waged." (Graeme Goldsworthy)

- **A wrong worldview**

Wrong worldviews or perspectives about your own or other people's behaviour, cultures, achievements, interpretations, beliefs, and their upbringing.

Human responses: Criticism, judging others, struggling to love all people, wrong motives.

CATEGORY 4: SERVING MULTIPLE MASTERS (IDOLS)

Scripture: Matthew 6:24

Displayed as: Selfish, prideful people who are inflated by their own ego.

They chase after temporary things and are deceived by ungodly motives. Money and wealth is very prominent in their approach towards life in general. They are very eager to control people and things and easily deceived by Satan's many schemes. It's interesting that the comparison Jesus made here is between God and Mammon. Money has caused many believers to become lukewarm in their devotion to God. We must know that money is an earthly currency and belongs to the decay of this world.

People who have idols in their lives always want to prove that they know better, do better or have achieved the best. They are dissatisfied with what they have and corrupt in their thinking and dealings with others. They always go out to please themselves first. Their motives in life are centred around themselves and they will struggle to allow God's kingdom to rule their hearts. They are very impulsive when making decisions. Disobedience is very prominent in their life, and they struggle to keep their commitments.

In Ezekiel 14:3 God says that He will not hear when there are idols in their hearts. Idols produce wrong motives and prevent God from answering our prayers (James 4:3).

Human responses: Greedy, stingy, arrogance, dominating others, unwillingness to reconcile with God and people, disobedient, unfaithful, lack of transparency with God and with others, wrong motives.

CATEGORY 5: ANXIETY OF LIFE

Scripture: Matthew 6:25-34

Displayed as: People who always feel they are left behind and forgotten by God. They struggle to accept God's blessings for them. They always want to compensate for things God and people give them out of love. They accept their current circumstances as permanent and struggle to trust God for breakthroughs. Full of fear, anxiety and worry about the future. They try to figure out their tomorrow without the presence and promises of God. They struggle to live in faith, and they are gripped by the present realities of life. These double-minded people with faithless prayers will have no power (Mark 6:5-6, James 1:6-8).

Human responses: worry, fearful, negative speech, hopelessness, depression, low self-esteem, lack of faith.

CATEGORY 6: OTHER GENERAL PRAYER OBSTACLES

There are a few obstacles that may also hinder prayer and sometimes it is because of spiritual immaturity and ignorance.

- Praying to God without going through His Son, Jesus Christ. (John 14:6)

- Praying while ignoring scripture. (Proverbs 28:9, 1 John 3:22)

- Praying to impress others. (Matthew 6:5-8)

- Praying while ignoring the poor. (Proverbs 21:13)

- Praying with selfish and lustful motives. (James 4:3)

- Praying without patience not realizing that we can't rush God. (Psalm 46:10)

- Praying prayers that are not in line with God's will. (1 John 5:14)

- Praying without repentance or praying with wickedness in our hearts. (Proverbs 15:29)

- Not making time to pray.

- Losing focus or getting distracted while praying.

All of these stumbling blocks can be overcome as we pursue more of Jesus in our lives and allow other disciples of Jesus to disciple us in praying without ignorance or disobedience.

THE GOSPEL IS THE ULTIMATE SOLUTION TO ALL OUR PROBLEMS

Yes, the Gospel is the solution to all our problems if we understand, believe, and apply it to our lives. Hallelujah! God wants to be our greatest treasure in life. Turn your heart to God, submit to His Lordship and make His kingdom your ultimate treasure. Hearing, believing, and applying the Gospel of Jesus Christ is the solution to all our unanswered prayers.

Only the power of the Holy Spirit can transform our hearts to being Christ-centered. The Holy Spirit will help us to prioritise God and His kingdom which will ultimately solve our problems and help us to overcome all of these stumbling blocks.

- Repent, renounce the wrong and receive God's forgiveness, allow Him to revive your spirit and to replace the lies with His truth.

- Resist the devil and stay away from places where your weaknesses are exposed to temptation.

- Seek and put God's kingdom first in your life and ask the Holy Spirit to fill you with the unconditional love of God.

- Learn to forgive immediately and to not keep record of people's wrongs.

- Look at your own heart first, before you judge others, and put yourself in their shoes to try to understand their errors.

- Spend enough time in the Word of God to cultivate a kingdom perspective.

- Praise Him for what He has promised to do for those who put their trust in Him. Jesus said that when we pray, we have to believe that He is able to help us, and not allow doubt in our hearts. Everything is possible with God.

- Commit to a weekly accountable personal discipleship with another disciple to mentor your spiritual growth.

- Pray and trust God for miraculous divine intervention in your life.

WE DON'T HAVE BECAUSE WE DON'T ASK OR PRAY

The answer to why we have unanswered and ineffective prayers can relate to many things, but I believe is ultimately found in the first five verses of James 4.

> *What causes quarrels and what causes fights among you? Is it not this, that your passions are at war within you? You desire and do not have, so you murder. You covet and cannot obtain, so you fight and quarrel. You do not have, because you do not ask. You ask and do not receive, because you ask wrongly, to spend it on your passions. You adulterous people! Do you not know that friendship with the world is enmity with God? Therefore whoever wishes to be a friend of the world makes himself an enemy of God. Or do you suppose it is to no purpose that the Scripture says, "He yearns jealously over the spirit that he has made to dwell in us"? James 4:1-5*

The Spirit of God yearns jealously for our full participation toward His complete inward work and calling in us. Living and abiding in friendship with the Almighty God is our destiny. Let me draw your attention to three short phrases in these Scriptures that point to the problem: you do not have; you do not ask, and you do not receive. Reading this, we suddenly find the reason behind the negative outcome; your passions are at war within you, you covet, you fight, quarrel and you ask wrongly to spend it on your passions. And then he finally nailed the truth. "Do you not know that friendship with the world is enmity with God?"

The same Greek word for "ask" is used in both Luke 11:9, when Jesus teaches His disciples about prayer and in James 4:2, when He rebukes the people of selfishness and lustful desires. He calls those who live outside an intimate friendship with God and are happy to do so, adulterous. This is how enmity with God is described. To conclude, we either live with intimacy or enmity with God. There is no alternative.

As children of the most high God, who are covenantally bound and intimately joined in friendship through the sacrificial blood of our Lord and Savior, Jesus Christ; we are commanded to live by faith, to have a faith filled mind and God-fearing heart, full of hope, faith and love. "The righteous shall live by faith!" (Romans 1:17) Therefore we should have heavenly confidence to ask, seek and knock at the heart of a loving Father to be helped in times of need for ourselves and other people. We should be eager and ready to approach Him and His throne of mercy and grace to ask for divine intervention in earthly matters.

I believe and I'm totally convinced that it is crucial for any church to have strong, established prayer within every aspect of their being.

It's time to overcome the stumbling blocks of ineffective prayer and rise to enjoy His awesome answers to our prayers.

Take a leap of faith and use any stumbling block to become a steppingstone towards a life of faith, as a son and daughter of a righteous and just God, our Creator. Let's walk in the light of Him who called us out of darkness unto His glorious light.

> Let's pray in times of difficulty!
>
> Let's pray in times of victory!
>
> Let's pray for more of Him to invade our hearts!
>
> Let's pray for those who don't know Him!
>
> Let's pray from a place of victory!
>
> Let's pray without ceasing!

"Prayer is the key that unlocks all the storehouses of God's infinite grace and power. All that God is, and all that God has, is at the disposal of prayer; but we must use the key. Prayer can do anything that God can do, and since God can do anything, prayer is omnipotent. No one can stand against the person who knows how to pray, who meets all the conditions of prevailing prayer, and who really prays. The Lord God Omnipotent works for him and through him." [17]

May we always remember that God is just a prayer away, a close friend in times of rejoicing and need.

> *"Therefore I want [desire] the men in every place to pray, lifting up holy hands, without anger [resentment] and disputing [strive] or quarreling [disagreement] or doubt [in their mind]."* *1 Timothy 2:8 (AMP)*

Let's Pray!

---

17   Torrey, Reuben A. The Power of Prayer and the Prayer of Power

APPLICATION

Write down three things you have learned from this Chapter:

____

____

____

____

Which truths have you learned that you will commit to apply in your devotion to God:

____

____

____

____

How and in what way will you apply this truth to your daily devotion?

____

____

____

____

Prayer:
Father, forgive me for all that I have harboured in my heart that has affected my communication and walk with you. Show me areas of my thinking and heart that hinder my prayers, in the name of Jesus. Amen.

Chapter 17

Practical guidance in prayer

Jesus portrayed something toward His disciple's concerning prayer in such a way that when they asked Him to teach them to pray, they knew exactly what it involved. They counted the cost in advance. Jesus' primary custom to pray was mostly early mornings but it extended through the day. Emotional highs or lows or even physical tiredness did not stop Him from praying.

THE BEST TIME TO PRAY

Although the Bible recommends that we pray without ceasing, there seems to be some moments where it is practically easier to pray. One of the best times to pray is first thing in the morning. With the current distractions in our society, you will have to be intentional and strategic if you want to develop a strong prayer life. In the scriptures, there were several hours of prayer observed during the day, but also many references towards early morning prayer. John Bunyan said:

"He who runs from God in the morning would scarcely find Him the rest of the day."

Most leaders have found it helpful to meet with God before the busyness of the day. Our motivation in making time to pray is of most importance. It's not supposed to be a 'to do' everyday but rather a 'should do' for all else to happen smoothly during our day. Let's look at a few scriptures to guide us in this matter.

Now in the morning, having risen a long while before daylight, He went out and departed to a solitary place; and there He prayed. Mark 1:35

From the Psalms of David during his times of joy, distress, and when he was in the wilderness of Judah.

O God, You are my God; Early will I seek You; My soul thirsts for You; My flesh longs for You In a dry and thirsty land Where there is no water."
Psalm 63:1 (NKJV)

My voice You shall hear in the morning, O Lord; In the morning I will direct it to You, And I will look up." Psalm 5:1-3

"Evening and morning and at noon I will pray, and cry aloud, And He shall hear my voice." Psalm 55:17

"But I will sing of Your power; Yes, I will sing aloud of Your mercy in the morning; For You have been my defence And refuge in the day of my trouble." Psalm 59:16

"But to You I have cried out, O LORD, And in the morning my prayer comes before You." Psalm 88:13

"Your people shall be volunteers In the day of Your power; In the beauties of holiness, from the womb of the morning, You have the dew of Your youth." Psalm 110:3

Edward McKendree Bounds said,

"I ought to pray before seeing anyone."

Robert Murray Mc Cheyne said this about morning prayer,

"In general, it is best to have at least one hour alone with God before engaging in anything else."

POSTURES OF PRAYER

Understanding postures of prayer is very important because we find many in the Bible. Abraham fell upon his face before God. (See Genesis 17:3, 17.) Moses prayed with his hands outstretched. (Exodus 9:27–29.) King Solomon knelt in prayer. (I Kings 8:54.) Jesus prayed looking up into heaven. (Mark 6:41, John 11:41, and 17:1.)

There is no one particularly correct way to pray. Communication with God does not require a certain physical position but using these postures when we pray can give expression to the attitudes of our hearts.

God is more interested in our heart's posture than our physical position. Here we will look at a list of different postures of prayer, discuss their symbolism and give scripture reference for it.

[Some content in this chapter was taken from free online resources.]

1. Lying prostrate on our faces before God

No position symbolizes humility better than being on our faces before God. This position of prayer demonstrates the beatitude of being poor in spirit. Lying prostrate before God expresses the following attitudes:

- It is an acknowledgement of our total unworthiness. (Genesis 17:3,17)

- It is recognition of the need for God's mercy. (Luke 5:12)

- It is the right response to a serious crisis. (Numbers 20:6, Joshua 7:6)

"He went a little farther and fell on His face, and prayed, saying, "O My Father, if it is possible, let this cup pass from Me; nevertheless, not as I will, but as You will." Matthew 26:39

When I saw him, I fell at his feet as though dead. Revelation 1:17a

2. Kneeling before God

Signifies surrender and repentance when we appeal to God for mercy and forgiveness. Kneeling before the Lord is a symbol of the heart attitude, we should have to make such a petition. A visual image of submission to His authority. It reflects the beatitude of mourning over sin and expresses the following attitudes:

- It acknowledges the Lordship of Jesus Christ. (Philippians 2:9-11)

- It is a sign of earnest appeal. (1 Kings 8:54, 18:41-46)

- It is a sign of personal humility. (Ps 95:6, Dan 6:10)

"But Peter put them all out, and knelt down and prayed. And turning to the body he said, "Tabitha, arise." And she opened her eyes, and when she saw Peter she sat up." Acts 9:40

"And when he had said these things, he knelt down and prayed with them all." Acts 20:36

3. Bowing before the Lord

One who bows before God conveys an attitude of honor, gratitude, and faith, acknowledging that all things come from His hand. When Job suffered great losses, he bowed down on the ground (Job 1:20–21). This position of prayer reflects the beatitude of meekness and expresses the following attitudes:

- It is a sign of reverence.

- It is an expression of worship.

  But the Lord, who brought you up from the land of Egypt with great power and with an outstretched arm, Him you shall fear, and to Him you shall bow yourselves down, and to Him you shall sacrifice. 2 Kings 17:36

  I will bow down toward Your holy temple. And give thanks to Your name for Your lovingkindness and Your truth; For You have magnified Your word according to all Your name. Psalm 138:2

  Humble yourselves in the presence of the Lord, and He will exalt you. James 4:10

  For this reason I bow my knees before the Father. Ephesians 3:14

4. Standing before the Lord

To stand before a ruler indicates that you have a legal right to be there. It is only through the righteousness of Jesus Christ that we can approach God as His children. It is also a position of reverence and honour – a sign of readiness to obey instructions. This position of prayer reflects the beatitude of hungering and thirsting for righteousness and expresses the following attitudes:

- It represents our position in Christ's righteousness (Romans 5:1–2, 1 Samuel 1:26).

- It symbolizes our preparation for battle. (Ephesians 6:13–18, Genesis 18:22).

- It shows readiness to serve. (Daniel 1:5, Revelations 8:1-4).

  But stay awake at all times, praying that you may have strength to escape all these things that are going to take place, and to stand before the Son of Man." Luke 21:36

And whenever you stand praying, if you have anything against anyone, forgive him, that your Father in heaven may also forgive you your trespasses."
Mark 11:25

5. Sitting before the Lord

This posture symbolises rest and readiness to execute. In Scripture, sitting is a position of authority. When the king or rulers of a city sat in their official places, they were in a position to rule and judge and to have their judgments carried out. This prayer position reflects the beatitude of giving and receiving mercy, and it expresses the following attitudes:

- It represents us resting in Him and being in awe of Him.
  (Matthew 11:28-30, 1 Chronicles 17:16-27)

- It reminds us that all believers are seated with Christ in heaven.
  (Ephesians 1:15–23 and 2:4–7.)

- It represents God's call to forgive offenders and cleansing ourselves
  (Matthew 6:14–15, Ephesians 4:31–32).

  But God, being rich in mercy, because of the great love with which he loved us, even when we were dead in our trespasses, made us alive together with Christ—by grace you have been saved— and raised us up with him and seated us with him in the heavenly places in Christ Jesus. Ephesians 2:4–6

6. Laying on our beds before the Lord

Another posture that communicates resting but also waiting on God's in silence for His intervention on our behalf. This position of prayer also demonstrates the beatitude of being poor in spirit, meditating on the goodness of God and the things of His Kingdom.

- It communicates a position of waiting, resting, stilling our hearts and minds, meditating and refuelling with the Lord.
  (Psalm 46:10, Luke 5:18-25)

- Showing our dependence on God to strengthen and heal us.
  (Matthew 9:2,6)

  Be angry, and do not sin. Meditate within your heart on your bed, and be still. Psalm 4:4 (NKJV)

There he found a man named Aeneas, bedridden for eight years, who was paralyzed. And Peter said to him, "Aeneas, Jesus Christ heals you; rise and make your bed." And immediately he rose. Acts 9:33-34

7. Walking and praying before the Lord

This posture symbolises communion with God but also presents us in a battle position before God against our adversaries. Walking has a way of intensifying your prayer and request before the Lord. This prayer position reflects the beatitude of standing against persecution and it expresses the following attitudes:

- Enjoying time and fellowship with God. (Genesis 3:8a)

- It represents an attitude of not giving up but continuing to walk in faith (2 Kings 4:35)

- Walking in God's promises and victory, ready to follow God in obedience. (Joshua 6:12-14)

By faith the people crossed the Red Sea as on dry land, but the Egyptians, when they attempted to do the same, were drowned. By faith the walls of Jericho fell down after they had been encircled for seven days. Hebrews 11:29-30

8. Raising of hands before the Lord

In the Scriptures, the outstretched arm was symbolic of seeking God's mercy and blessing. It speaks of surrender, no hidden agenda, and a disposition of praise. It represents God prevailing against the enemy when Moses left Egypt and when he fought against the Amalekites. A call unto people to remember the mighty works of God. This position of prayer reflects the beatitude of being a peacemaker and expresses the following attitudes.

- It appeals to God's sovereign power. (Exodus 9:29, 17:11)

- It reflects God's redeeming work: salvation. (Deuteronomy 7:18-19)

- It demonstrates worship and petitions God's blessing. (1 Kings 8:22-23,28-29)

"I desire therefore that the men pray everywhere, lifting up holy hands, without wrath and doubting;" 1 Timothy 2:8

"Thus I will bless You while I live; I will lift up my hands in Your name." Psalm 63:4

"So Moses said to him, "As soon as I have gone out of the city, I will spread out my hands to the LORD; the thunder will cease, and there will be no more hail, that you may know that the earth is the LORD'S." Exodus 9:29

9. Uplifted faces with open/closed eyes turned towards God

Looking up to heaven with open or closed eyes draws our attention from earthly to heavenly realities. This is a posture of showing our delight in Him. We are not alone. God is watching us. This life is not all there is – think on eternity perspectives. This posture represents an attitude of:

- Dependence on God, a hunger and thirst for His justice and righteousness in our lives.

- A seeking after God's blessing.

- An expectation after the power and purity of the Holy Spirit.

To you I lift up my eyes, O you who are enthroned in the heavens! Behold, as the eyes of servants look to the hand of their master, as the eyes of a maidservant to the hand of her mistress, so our eyes look to the LORD our God, till he has mercy upon us. Psalm 123:1-2 AMP

And looking up to heaven, he sighed and said to him, "Ephphatha," that is, "Be opened."' Mark 7:34

Taking the five loaves and two fish and looking up to heaven, he gave thanks and broke the loaves. Mark 6:41

After Jesus said this, he looked toward heaven and prayed. John 17:1

10. Different emotional expressions unto God

Leaping, crying, shouting or silent waiting. An expression of the heart's emotions whether from joy to awe.

This poor man cried out, and the Lord heard him, And saved him out of all his troubles. Psalm 34:6 (NKJV)

Now Hannah spoke in her heart; only her lips moved, but her voice was not heard. Therefore Eli thought she was drunk. 1 Samuel 1:13 (NKJV)

The posture you assume while praying should be determined by how you feel your spirit is directing you to. Sometimes, you will find that your posture at the start of your prayer is different from your posture by the time you finish. Just be flexible and allow the Holy Spirit to guide you.

FASTING

Fasting is a human action for consecrating themselves to God and His service. An outward demonstration of trusting in Him for breakthroughs and answers. Fast is not something we can use to impress or manipulate God. The main purpose of fast is for us to turn our reverence and focus to Him as we wait for His salvation.

There are many fasts which are an abomination to God because of its motivation and attitude. The effect of these fasts will cause God to not listen to our voices (Isaiah 58:4b). The God-honouring fast is a fast of inward devotion to God. This fast that pleases God has many benefits in advancing God's kingdom but ultimately it is that our prayers are heard (Isaiah 58:9). The outcomes of a God-pleasing fast are described in Isaiah 58:11-12:

> *And the LORD will guide you continually and satisfy your desire in scorched places and make your bones strong; and you shall be like a watered garden, like a spring of water, whose waters do not fail. And your ancient ruins shall be rebuilt; you shall raise up the foundations of many generations; you shall be called the repairer of the breach, the restorer of streets to dwell in.*

TO WHOM DO WE PRAY?

The entire Godhead is involved in prayer, but it is important to appreciate the different roles that they play with regards to prayer. Primarily, prayer is addressed to God the Father, in the name of Jesus, by the help of the Holy Spirit. We pray to the Father in the name of Jesus.

> *But when you pray, go into your room and shut the door and pray to your Father who is in secret. Matthew 6:6*

"To pray, then, in the name of Jesus Christ, simply means that we recognize that we have no claims whatsoever on God. We recognize that we have no merit whatsoever in His sight, and furthermore, we recognize that Jesus Christ has immeasurable claims on God and has given us the right to draw near to God, not based on our claims, but on the basis of His claims.

When we thus draw near to God in prayer, God will give us what we ask. Prayer in the name of Jesus Christ prevails with God." [18]

> *Whatever you ask in my name, this I will do, that the Father may be glorified in the Son. John 14:13*

Although all members of the Godhead can receive worship, we find that Jesus overwhelmingly teaches us to address our prayers to the Father. We are not told to address prayer to Jesus and don't say it is wrong. We are told to pray in the Name of Jesus to the Father because we approach the throne of God through the finish work of the cross. Jesus is the way to the Father and everything about Jesus should direct our hearts to the Father. Neither are we taught to address prayer to the Holy Spirit. That does not mean that if someone calls on Jesus, he will not be heard. He that calls on the name of the Lord shall be saved. The call for salvation is different from other prayers.

> *Jesus said to him, "I am the way, and the truth, and the life. No one comes to the Father except through me. John 14:6*

"Do you realize that we honor the name of Christ by asking great things in His name? Do you realize that we dishonour that name by not daring to ask great things in His name? Oh, have faith in the power of Jesus' name, and dare to ask great things in His name." [19]

Let's Pray!

---

18   Torrey, Reuben A. The Power of Prayer and the Prayer of Power
19   Torrey, Reuben A. The Power of Prayer and the Prayer of Power

APPLICATION

Write down three things you have learned from this Chapter:

____

____

____

____

Which truths have you learned that you will commit to apply in your devotion to God:

____

____

____

____

How and in what way will you apply this truth to your daily devotion?

____

____

____

____

Prayer:
Heavenly Father, I commit to a lifestyle of prayer. Help me to remain faithful, in the mighty name of Jesus Christ. Lord, help me to stay committed to praying for myself and others and not become weary in following you. Amen.

Chapter **18**

Different prayers

DIFFERENT PRAYERS

A VISION FOR PRAYER

The purpose of this book is not to give a detailed teaching on all the benefits, difficulties, or methods for successful prayer, but rather a helping tool to teach people how to pray; to enjoy answered prayers, and to discover how to advance God's kingdom through prayer. In a nutshell, *'Effective prayer is the application of Biblical truth to what we believe.'*

It is a spiritual blessing and inheritance, a conversation between God and mankind. God initiates on mankind's behalf the restoration of all things through heavenly intervention to establish a partnership with mankind for the greatest, redemptive work of God on the earth.

God's redemptive work on earth through Jesus was not just to restore a relationship, but also a people that will impact the generations after them. The vision of heaven the apostle John saw was about:

> *And one of the elders said to me, "Weep no more; behold, The Lion of the tribe of Judah, the Root of David, who conquered. Between the throne and the four living creatures and among the elders he saw a Lamb standing, as though it had been slain, with seven horns and with seven eyes, which are the seven spirits of God sent out into all the earth. And he went and took the scroll from the right hand of him who was seated on the throne. And when he had taken the scroll, the four living creatures and the twenty-four elders fell down before the Lamb, each holding a harp, and golden bowls full of incense, which are the prayers of the saints. And they sang a new song, saying, Worthy are you to take the scroll and to open its seals, for you were slain, and by your blood you ransomed people for God from every tribe and language and people and nation, and you have made them a kingdom and priests to our God, and they shall reign on the earth. Revelation 5:5-10*

God's plan of restoration is seen as a golden thread throughout history and will finally end in heaven at the wedding of the bride and the bridegroom. It will be the greatest love reunion ever, between mankind and God.

> *After this I will return, and I will rebuild the tent of David that has fallen; I will rebuild its ruins, and I will restore it, that the remnant of mankind may seek the Lord, and all the Gentiles who are called by my name, says the Lord, who makes these things known from of old. Acts 15:16-18*

This is the ultimate goal - more people worshiping before the throne of God, admiring the Lamb with true honesty. Casting their crowns before the one who deserves all honor and glory. If our prayers are not about more of Him, what will it involve?

DIFFERENT TYPES OF PRAYER

Having a vibrant prayer life is often cited as a significant spiritual practice among followers of Jesus. Scripture affirms the concept of praying not only individually, but also as a community. Praying with others becomes a powerful way to lift our voices to the Lord and to share our petitions with God as the body of Christ. When we pray, we often do so by ourselves, but we are encouraged to pray with others, as well. Jesus said:

> *For where two or three are gathered in my name, there am I among them.*
> *Matthew 18:20*

Prayer is powerful, it is intimate, and it changes the hearts of those who pray regularly by drawing us closer to God. All prayers should be done with faith (Mark 9:23; 11:23) in the name of Jesus Christ to the Lord God Almighty on a personal or corporate level. Prayer is happening in the spiritual realm and is fuelled by faith.

When we agree with others in corporate prayer it will be more powerful and effective because one will put a thousand to flight and two will put ten thousand to flight (Joshua 23:10; Deuteronomy 32:30). There are different types of prayer, and we find evidence of this in the Bible. Some prayers may be motivated by a need for healing, help, or a grateful heart. Other prayers are a result of considering and declaring the magnificence of God.

Fervent prayers

The apostles and disciples in the first church in Acts understood fervent prayers very well. Their commitment to advance the kingdom of God was more important than the safety of their lives. Their faith in God's promises was firmly settled and their conviction to trust Him to the ultimate extent was evident in many places in the book of Acts.

In chapter 12, we find the disciples in the midst of persecution and the apostle James were killed while the apostle Peter was put into jail. But the church:

So Peter was kept in prison, but earnest prayer for him was made to God by the church. Acts 12:5

The words '*earnest prayer*' in this verse is translated in other Bible versions with; fervent, constant, nonstop, ongoing, and intense intercession. [AMPC, KJV]. From the original text ('*ektenos*') meaning to be '*intensely*' coming from a verb which means '*to stretch out the hand*', thus it means to be stretched out - earnest, resolute, tense [Strong's].

You also must help us by prayer, so that many will give thanks on our behalf for the blessing granted us through the prayers of many. 2 Corinthians 1:11

Effective prayer is not about the words we use nor the time we spend but the heart we apply. (PW Coffee)

Making intercession

"When we intercede in prayer, we stand in the gap between God's righteousness and the error of man." Stormie O'Martian

The power of prayer has been limited for too long in the lives of believers and mostly used for personal needs. It's time to unite as children of God in different ways to intercede for heavenly intervention in our world. It's time to arise and to fight as an army from a place of victory, against the forces of darkness, for the salvation of mankind. The battle has been won through Jesus and we must enforce this victory on earth.

*Consequently, he is able to save to the uttermost those who draw near to God through him, **since he always lives to make intercession for them**. Hebrew 7:25*

Intercession in the Bible was the work of priests. In Christ we are called as priests to follow in His example. Making intercession means to mediate, to go between, or plead for another through prayer, petition, or entreaty in favour of another. It is a ministry in the body of Christ that is most important and significant, however largely unseen, but God looks for those who will stand up and intercede on behalf of others.

And I sought for a man among them who should build up the wall and stand in the breach before me for the land, that I should not destroy it, but I found none. Ezekiel 22:30

Importantly, the journey into intercession is one of relationship and friendship with God. The closer we walk with God the more His love for us and others abounds and moves us to intercede for the things that concern Him regarding His kingdom and the destiny of man; and to appeal through intercession the victory of Jesus Christ that was established in heaven.

I urge, then, first of all, that requests, prayers, intercession and thanksgiving be made for everyone, for kings and all who are in high positions, that we may lead a peaceful and quiet life, godly and dignified in every way. This is good, and it is pleasing in the sight of God our Savior, who desires all people to be saved and to come to the knowledge of the truth. 1 Timothy 2:1

Churches have to have a vision to become powerhouses of prayer, who influence the kingdom of this world with the kingdom of God.

Praying for the Lost

Have you ever heard of Dr Larry Lea and The Church on the Rock in Rockwall, Texas? Within five years from 1980, the congregation had increased to over 5,000 in 1986. It is said that one of the main reasons for this phenomenal growth was because of the prayer culture in the church. Many people came weekly to accept Jesus as their Saviour and it was attributed to a specific prayer the congregation prayed at their weekly gatherings. The combined *"Prayer for the lost"* was articulated from these scriptures.

But this is a people plundered and looted; they are all of them trapped in holes and hidden in prisons they have become plunder with none to rescue, spoil with none to say, "Restore!" Isaiah 42:22

I will say to the north, Give up, and to the south, Do not withhold; bring my sons from afar and my daughters from the end of the earth, everyone who is called by my name, whom I created for my glory, whom I formed and made." Bring out the people who are blind, yet have eyes, who are deaf, yet have ears! Isaiah 43:6-9

And people will come from east and west, and from north and south, and recline at table in the kingdom of God. And behold, some are last who will be first, and some are first who will be last. Luke 13:29

Then he said to his disciples, "The harvest is plentiful, but the laborers are few; therefore pray earnestly to the Lord of the harvest to send out laborers into his harvest." Matthew 9:38

It is definitely God's will to pray for the harvest of souls and the laborers in the fields. Calling for the prodigals to come home and those who don't know Jesus Christ to come to the full knowledge of His salvation through repentance.

This kind of prayer is conceived out of a deep compassion. When we intercede for lost people to be restored in their eternal identity and destiny, we position ourselves in the gap of the divide and plead for their complete reconciliation. We contend in faith while we feel the emotions and with a vision of their restored future. Prophetically we speak words of life that are stronger than death as we hear and foresee them to become. It's the compelling love of God reaching out through us in action.

To pray earnestly means to pray with intense earnestness, it's unceasing prevailing prayer, stretching out to God's presence with intense conviction for His interventions. *"It represents the soul stretched out in the intensity of its earnestness toward God."* [20]

Similar prayers done months and years before crusades in ancient revivals was part of the history of the evangelical church worldwide. Here is a short report from a revival in Australia:

A lady in Melbourne had read a book on prayer and had been very deeply impressed by one short sentence in the book: *"Pray through."* She had gone to work and had organized prayer meetings all over the city before we reached the place. Indeed, when we reached Melbourne, we found that there were 1,700 neighbourhood prayer meetings being held every week in Melbourne. We remained in that city four weeks.

During the first two weeks, the meetings were held by many different pastors and evangelists in some forty or fifty different centre's throughout the city, though meetings for the whole city were held at one o'clock, two o'clock, and three o'clock each day in the town hall. The last two weeks, the meetings were all concentrated in the Exposition Hall, which seated about eight thousand people. At the very first meeting in the Exposition Hall, the crowd was so large that they were swept by the police before them and packed the building far beyond its proper capacity, and there were large crowds still who could not get in. During those four weeks, 8,642 people made a definite profession of having accepted the Lord Jesus Christ as their Saviour.

---

20 Torrey, Reuben A. The Power of Prayer and the Prayer of Power

The report of what God had done in Melbourne spread not only all over Australia, but to India, England, Scotland, and Ireland, and resulted in a wonderful work of God in the leading cities of England, Scotland and Ireland.

The Great Welsh Revival in 1904 started as a prayer meeting and prayer began to go up all over England, Scotland, and Wales that God would send a revival not only to Cardiff, but to all Wales. When we reached Cardiff, we learned that a prayer meeting had been held for almost a year from six to seven every morning in Penarth, a suburb of Cardiff. The people had been praying for a great revival. These prayer warrior disciples and intercessors believed as follows when they prayed:

"Prayer will reach down into the deepest depths of sin and ruin and take hold of men and women who seem lost beyond all possibility or hope of redemption, and will lift them up until they are made ready for a place beside the Son of God upon the throne." [21]

WATCHMEN ON THE WALL

Jesus is the greatest example of intercession. After He paid the price for the salvation of all mankind, He returned to heaven to be crowned as the King of kings and Lord of lords, then He also took it on Himself to engage in intercession for all people (Hebrews 7:25). To watch and pray is to be continually in a state of awareness as a 'Watchman on the Wall.'

The salvation of all people is God's eternal desire, and for all to come to repentance and turn to Him.

The Lord is not slow to fulfill his promise as some count slowness, but is patient toward you, not wishing that any should perish, but that all should reach repentance. 2 Peter 3:9

This scripture is found in the context of a discussion on Jesus' second return. God will postpone His return for more people to repent and come to Him. His heart is after people coming to know Him. The prophet Isaiah is reporting how the Lord commanded him to put watchmen on the walls to do two things; to **listen** and to **watch**. Without watchmen on our walls or without watching we are open targets and unguarded. The worst scenario is to have watchmen in place who are ineffective in listening and watching.

---

21   Torrey, Reuben A. The Power of Prayer and the Prayer of Power

They are like dogs ineffective in guarding the premises.

For thus the Lord said to me: "Go, set a watchman; let him announce what he sees. When he sees riders, horsemen in pairs, riders on donkeys, riders on camels, let him listen diligently, very diligently." Isaiah 21:6-7

His watchmen are blind; they are all without knowledge; they are all silent dogs; they cannot bark, dreaming, lying down, loving to slumber.
Isaiah 56:10

Now is a time to put watchmen in place and let them guard the beloved premises of God. A praying, interceding church who have watchmen on their walls, and have people in their daily conversations with God is a church that prepares themselves for a mighty revival from God's Spirit. God loves it when we prioritize what He prioritizes first.

Watchmen are prayer warriors standing in the gap between a righteous God and the errors of mankind; prophetic intercessors who remind God daily of His promises toward His people. They are mounted warriors on behalf of the mandate of God, positioned to bring to pass the glory of God through prayer.

On your walls, O Jerusalem, I have set watchmen; all the day and all the night they shall never be silent. You who put the LORD in remembrance, take no rest, and give him no rest until he establishes Jerusalem and makes it a praise in the earth. Isaiah 62:6-7

We should always be aware that our battles are spiritual and not physical, against the powers of darkness and not the flesh. We can stop many battles and evil attacks by being watchful and by positioning watchmen on our walls. Through proactive prayers and watchmen that are involved in fighting battles before they appear we will have spiritual victories before they are recognized. Thank God that He has given us weapons ready for the fight. This is how a *'House of Prayer'* operates.

Who will answer the call to be a watchman on the walls of the last days churches?

For thus the Lord said to me: "Go, set a watchman; let him announce what he sees.... Then he who saw cried out: "Upon a watchtower I stand, O Lord, continually by day, and at my post I am stationed whole nights. Isaiah 21:6, 8

Let's Pray!

APPLICATION

Write down three things you have learned from this Chapter:

____

____

____

____

Which truths have you learned that you will commit to apply in your devotion to God:

____

____

____

____

How and in what way will you apply this truth to your daily devotion?

____

____

____

____

Prayer:
Father God, please deposit a vision of prayer in my heart to continue to live in deep intimacy with You. Grant in me a spirit of fervent prayer. Amen.

Appendix

Type	Description	Prayer Content	Scripture
1	Prayer of Adoration.	Worship to God for who He is, admiring His awe.	Revelation 5:12; 19:7; Psalm 29:2
2	Prayer of Praise & Thanksgiving.	Praise and thanksgiving for what He has done.	1 Chronicles 16:34-35; Psalms overall
3	Prayer of Faith Declaration.	Making faith declarations about the character of God, his promises and power to people.	Romans 10:8; Hebrews 11:3
4	Prayer of Petition or Supplication.	Asking God for supplying in our our daily requests and needs.	Philippians 4:6; Ephesians 6:18
5	Prayer of Consecration.	Consecrate yourselves and others to God for His service.	Matthew 26:39; Joshua 3:5, Acts 13:2-3
6	Prayer of Transformation and Sanctification.	Personal purification and sanctification before God.	Psalm 139:23-24
7	Prayer of Confession and Repentance.	Repenting from our sins and confessing our sins before Him and others to receive forgiveness of our sins.	Psalm 32:5; 1 John 1:9
8	Prayer of Salvation.	Inviting Jesus as your Saviour and Lord when accepting Him.	Romans 10:1,9-13
9	Prayer of Forgiveness.	Forgiving others for their sins against you and the deliverance of offences.	Luke 6:36-37
10	Prayer for Deliverance and Freedom from Idols.	Prayer of freedom from addictions, slavery and idol worship.	2 Corinthians 6:14-18; 1 Thessalonians 1:9; Psalm 107:6
11	Prayer of Healing.	Healing of the sick and sickness.	James 5:15; Psalm 107:20; Jeremiah 17:14
12	Prayer of Intercession.	Standing in the gap for other people's needs and salvation.	1 Timothy 2:1; Hebrews 7:25 John 17
13	Spiritual Warfare.	Warfare against the principalities and powers of darkness.	Ephesians 6:12,18
14	Prayer of Vows.	Vowing promises to God that you will keep in future.	1 Samuel 1:10-11
15	Prayer of Blessing.	Blessing over ourselves and other people.	Philippians 1:9-11 Numbers 6:24-26

CRAFTED PRAYERS: Examples of prayers to be used in personal prayer times.

Praise: Psalm 145:1-3
Heavenly Father, I want to praise you and exalt your name above all others for what you have done for me. You are my God and King, and I express admiration and praise of your name forever and ever. I will praise you every day; yes, I will praise you forever. Great are You Lord! You are most worthy of praise! No one can measure Your greatness. Amen"

Worship: Revelation 4:8-11
Heavenly Father, I bow before you in worship. I cry, 'Holy, holy, holy are You, Lord God, the Almighty One, who was and who is and who is to come. Worthy are You, my Lord and God, to receive the glory and the honor and the power; for You created all things. I worship You with my whole life. Amen.

Salvation: Joel 2:32
Jesus, I come before You and acknowledge that You are Lord. I am a sinner in need of salvation. Please forgive me of all my sin and come and be my Saviour and Lord. I believe You died in my place, rose from the dead and ascended to Heaven and have now taken me from the Kingdom of darkness into Your Kingdom of light. Thank you for saving me and transforming my life. In Jesus Name, amen.

Baptism of the Holy Spirit: Luke 11:10,13
Heavenly Father, thank you that Jesus came to baptise us with the Holy Spirit and fire. Thank you for giving the Holy Spirit to those who ask. Therefore, I ask you Lord Jesus please baptise me with Your Holy Spirit, now. I receive it by faith in Your Word and in the Name of Jesus. Help me to live this new life as you want, come and continue to fill me with more of Your Spirit, amen.

Forgiveness for others: Matthew 6:14-15
Heavenly Father, I come to you in the name of Jesus and want to forgive ______________ (name) for ______________________ (wrong against me), because You have forgiven me my wrong doings (sin). Help me to always have a forgiving heart towards others. I release them from the prison I have kept them in. Give me the strength to forgive when I find it hard to. In Jesus Name, amen.

Needs/Provision: Matthew 33:32-33

Heavenly Father, I acknowledge that You know of my need for food to eat, water to drink and clothes to wear and a dwelling place to have. And as I seek first and most importantly after Your kingdom and righteousness, I can trust that in all these things I have need of, will be given to me. Thank you for Your provision that comes through the labour of my hands as I seek to do Your will. In Jesus Name, amen."

Temptation: Corinthians 10:13

Heavenly Father, thank you that You are faithful, and you will not allow me to be tempted beyond what I am able to bear, and You make the way of escape, and give me the strength to be able to bear it. Lord, I am being tempted by Satan to ___________________. Please Lord, come and help me to escape and not give in to temptation. In Jesus Name, amen.

Wisdom: Proverbs 3:5-7

Heavenly Father, help me to trust in You, Lord, with all of my heart and mind, and not to rely on my own understanding. Help me to grow in wisdom and understanding as I acknowledge You in every aspect of my life. I thank You that as I do so I can trust You to direct my steps. Help me not to be wise in my own eyes, to rather fear You and avoid all evil things. In Jesus Name, amen.

Work: Ephesians 2:10

Heavenly Father, thank you that I am Your workmanship created in Jesus to do good works. You have placed within me gifts and abilities to be used in my life. Help me to discover what these are and use them for Your glory in my work, vocation and/or career. I also want to pray for those who are poor and jobless. Lord, please provide for them. Help me to experience work satisfaction and to see it as a means of You fulfilling my needs. In Jesus Name, amen.

Repentance: Luke 11:4

Heavenly Father, I come before You in the name of Jesus and confess I have sinned against You in this manner ___________________. Please forgive ___________________ and help me turn away from it and do what is right in Your sight. In Jesus Name, amen.

The Lost: 1 Timothy 2:4-6

Heavenly Father, You desire for all men to be saved and to come to know the truth that You are the one God and given only one Mediator between God and men, Christ Jesus. I ask in Jesus' name to reveal this truth to ________________ so that they may come to the saving knowledge of who Jesus is. Reveal unto them your love and bring someone along their path that will share the Gospel of Jesus Christ with them. In Jesus Name, amen.

Church and Church Leaders: Colossians 1:9-14

Heavenly Father, I ask that You fill the Church (local, national, global) with the knowledge of Your will in all wisdom and spiritual understanding; that the Church may walk worthy of You, fully pleasing You, being fruitful in every good work and increasing in the knowledge of God; strengthened with all might, according to Your glorious power, for all patience and longsuffering with joy; giving thanks to You who has qualified them to be partakers of the inheritance of the saints in the light of God. You have delivered them from the power of darkness and journeyed with them into the kingdom of the Son of Your love, in whom we have redemption through His blood, the forgiveness of sins. In Jesus Name, amen.

Nations and those in Authority: Psalm 2:8-12

Heavenly Father, Jesus has asked You to give Him the nations for His inheritance, and the ends of the earth for His possession. I pray for ________________ (nation); for the rulers and judges of this nation to be wise, ruling with fear of You, to be instructed by Your Word, to serve You in leading their nations with justice, to rejoice with trembling. I ask too that they come to a saving knowledge of Jesus Christ. Blessed is the nation that puts its trust in You. In Jesus Name, amen.

Enemies: Matthew 5:44

Heavenly Father, I bring before you; my 'enemy' and those to oppose me, those who judge me wrongly, and those who persecute me. Help me to love my enemy and do good things for them. Open their eyes and hearts to receive the love I give them, Lord, and I forgive those who say bad things about and bless them with eternal life. Please reveal the truth of Jesus Christ to them. In Jesus Name, amen"

Spiritual Growth: Ephesians 1:17-19 (Amplified)

Heavenly Father, you are the Father of glory. Please give me a spirit of wisdom and of revelation into the true knowledge of Who You are. I ask that the eyes of my heart may be flooded with light by the Holy Spirit, so that I will know and cherish the hope, the divine guarantee, the confident expectation to which You have called me. That I may know the riches of Your glorious inheritance in the saints. And that I will begin to know what the immeasurable and unlimited and surpassing greatness of Your active, spiritual power is in me. Thank you for doing this in accordance with the working of Your mighty strength. In Jesus Name, amen.

Healing: James 5:15

Heavenly Father, You are our Healer, our Divine doctor. I lift_______________ before You and with the prayer of faith, pray for their healing from ________________. Thank you for their healing as You say You will save the sick, and You will raise them up. You said that the fervent prayer of a righteous person has great power, therefore I command sickness to leave. In Jesus Name, amen.

Trials: James 1:2-4

Heavenly Father, thank you for my trials. Help me to consider it with joy that I am going through this trial because you say that in it You will help me overcome it. You say this testing of my faith produces patience, endurance, perseverance. And when this has its perfect work in me, I will be mature and complete, and in lack of nothing. Help me to trust Your process and to be content in what I have. In Jesus Name, amen.

Deliverance from the evil one: James 4:7-8

Heavenly Father, I submit to You and come under the finished work of the Blood of Jesus. I resist you, devil, and your schemes in the Mighty Name of my Lord and God, Jesus Christ. We overcome you Satan by the blood of the Lamb and you need to obey, so flee. Thank you Father that I can draw near to You and that You have delivered me. In Jesus Name, amen.

Our daily prayer: Psalm 19:14

Search me, O God, and know my heart! Try me and know my thoughts! Show me the obstacles that grieve you and lead me in the way everlasting! Let the words of my mouth and the meditation of my heart be acceptable in your sight, O LORD, my rock and my redeemer.

Peace: Romans: 15:13
Heavenly Father, You are my hope, my peace and my shelter. I will say to the LORD, "My refuge and my fortress, my God, in whom I trust." For he will deliver me from the snare of the fowler and from the deadly pestilence. He will cover me with his pinions, and under his wings I will find refuge; his faithfulness is a shield and buckler. Therefore, I will not fear the terror of the night, nor the arrow that flies by day. Please fill me with all joy and peace so that I may have a large amount of hope by the power of Your Holy Spirit. Lord, you are my Peace. In Jesus Name, amen.

Injustice: Deuteronomy 32:13-5
Heavenly Father, I ascribe greatness to You, my God. You are the Rock, Your work is perfect; all Your ways are justice, You are a God of truth and without injustice; You are Righteous and upright. Please intervene in this unjust _____________________ (situation, circumstance, event) and bring Your truth, justice and righteousness in that ________________ (situation, circumstance, event). In Jesus Name, amen.

Protection: Psalm 18:1-3
Heavenly Father, O Lord, You are my strength. You are my rock and my fortress and my deliverer; You are My God, my strength, in whom I will trust; You are my shield and the horn of my salvation, my stronghold. I call upon You, Lord, who is worthy to be praised; And You save me from my enemies. I ask for Your protection from ______________. You promised that those who dwell in the shelter of the Most High will abide in the shadow of the Almighty. I thank you for your protection and that you will command your angels concerning me to guard me in all your ways. In Jesus Name, amen."

Labourers in the harvest fields: Matthew 9:38
Heavenly Father, I pray for more laborers in the harvest fields and for lost people to come to know you personally. I pray specifically for _______ ______________________________ (names). Jesus, you said there are great quantities of people who are ready to hear the Good News, but the laborers are few, and not enough. Therefore, I ask You Lord to raise up and send out Your messengers into the world so all of mankind can hear the Good News. I pray for open doors where the Word of God is shared. I pray for the encouragement of the Spirit in the hearts of many missionaries. I pray for all generations to come to the full knowledge of Jesus Christ and His love for them. In Jesus Name, amen.

(These crafted prayers were compiled by Julie-Ann Bartleet)

Other
BOOKS
By the Authors

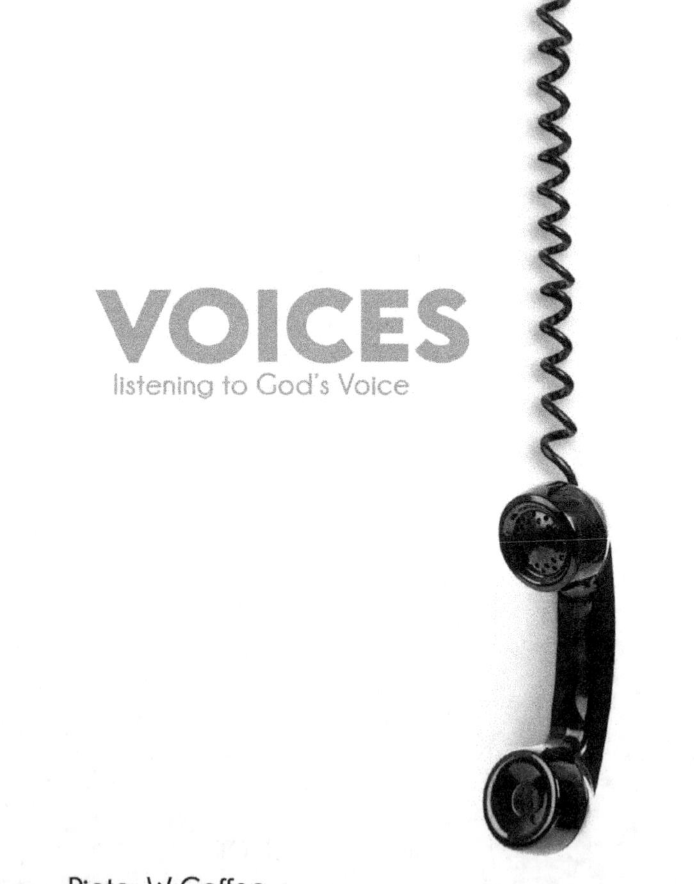
VOICES
listening to God's Voice
Pieter W Coffee

SUPERNATURAL IMMUNITY

**EXPLORING
GOD'S PROTECTIVE
POWER** FROM
PSALM 91 & MORE

ERIC BAPETEL